Antiracist Teacher Education

Antiracist Teacher Education

Theory and Practice

Volume 1

Edited by
Gilda Martínez-Alba
Luis Javier Pentón Herrera
Afra Ahmed Hersi

ROWMAN & LITTLEFIELD
Lanham • Boulder • New York • London

Published by Rowman & Littlefield
An imprint of The Rowman & Littlefield Publishing Group, Inc.
4501 Forbes Boulevard, Suite 200, Lanham, Maryland 20706
www.rowman.com

86-90 Paul Street, London EC2A 4NE

Copyright © 2022 by Gilda Martínez-Alba, Luis Javier Pentón Herrera, and Afra Ahmed Hersi

All rights reserved. No part of this book may be reproduced in any form or by any electronic or mechanical means, including information storage and retrieval systems, without written permission from the publisher, except by a reviewer who may quote passages in a review.

British Library Cataloguing in Publication Information Available

Library of Congress Cataloging-in-Publication Data

Names: Martinez-Alba, Gilda, editor. | Pentón Herrera, Luis Javier, editor. | Hersi, Afra, editor.
Title: Antiracist teacher education : theory and practice / Edited by Gilda Martinez-Alba, Luis Javier Penton Herrera, and Afra Hersi.
Description: Lanham : Rowman & Littlefield, [2022] | Includes bibliographical references.
Identifiers: LCCN 2022020746 (print) | LCCN 2022020747 (ebook) |
  ISBN 9781475865561 (cloth) | ISBN 9781475865578 (paperback) |
  ISBN 9781475865585 (ebook)
Subjects: LCSH: Teachers—Training of. | Multicultural education—Study and teaching. | Racism in education. | Social justice and education.
Classification: LCC LB1707 .A68 2022 (print) | LCC LB1707 (ebook) |
  DDC 370.71/1—dc23/eng/20220622
LC record available at https://lccn.loc.gov/2022020746
LC ebook record available at https://lccn.loc.gov/2022020747

Contents

Acknowledgments   vii

An Introduction to Antiracist Teacher Education: Theory into Practice   ix
Gilda Martínez-Alba, Luis Javier Pentón Herrera, and Afra Ahmed Hersi

1. Grounding Antiracism and Guiding Educators Beginning with Self   1
   Nancy P. Gallavan

2. Situating the Self in Context: Co-teaching to Prepare Antiracist Teachers to Teach in Urban Settings   19
   Laura Renzi and Matthew Kruger-Ross

3. L.I.S.T.E.N. Up: Antibias/Antiracist Orientations in Teacher Education   33
   Danné E. Davis and Sumi Hagiwara

4. Diversity, Equity, and Inclusion Matter: Preparing Teacher Candidates to Become Activist Educators   51
   Benita R. Brooks, Ramona T. Pittman, Jaime Coyne, Tori Hollas, and Mae Lane

5. Making Space for Critical Thought amid State Prohibitions: Critical Race Theory as a Framework to Inform Course Design and Student Learning Objectives   67
   Marisol Diaz, Sarah M. Straub, Tonya D. Jeffery, and Brian Uriegas

6. Cross-Pollinating Teacher Preparation: Antiracist Inclusive Lesson Planning in Writers' Workshop   81
   Amy Tondreau, Laurie Rabinowitz, and Zachary T. Barnes

7 A Curriculum of Accomplicity: Foundations, Concepts, and Actions for Justice Work in Education 101
Morna McDermott McNulty

8 Combating Anti-Asian Bias by Developing Intercultural Maturity through a Short-Term Study Abroad Program in China 121
Ashley Lucas and Xiaoming Liu

About the Editors 141

About the Contributors 143

Acknowledgments

We are grateful for the Association of Teacher Educators' (ATE) sponsorship and for the ATE Diversity Committee's support. We would also like to thank the authors who contributed to this book. Their vast knowledge and expertise are such incredible assets to the field.

An Introduction to Antiracist Teacher Education

Theory into Practice

Gilda Martínez-Alba, Luis Javier Pentón Herrera, and Afra Ahmed Hersi

Systemic racism, rooted in structural and institutional inequalities, continues to have devastating effects on People of Color (POC). Most recently, the tragic killings of George Floyd, Breonna Taylor, Ahmaud Arbery, and others have brought our nation's attention to the plight of the Black community. Meanwhile, racism against the Asian community has also increased exponentially since the outbreak of COVID-19 in 2020. We are once again reminded of the presence and ugliness of racism and racial injustice in our society. Racism and racial injustice not only hurt POC but also every member of our society. Therefore, it is time to join in solidarity and take action to tackle racism so that our nation truly embodies the ideal of having liberty and justice for all. The changing demographics in U.S. classrooms speak to the urgency of schools and teachers addressing the diversities among our students and providing equitable instruction to support the learning of all students. According to the National Center of Educational Statistics (Hussar et al., 2020), a significant shift in the composition of public school students occurred between fall 2000 and fall 2017. The percentage of White students decreased from 61 to 48%, and the percentage of Black students decreased from 17 to 15%. Meanwhile, the Hispanic student population increased from 16 to 27%, and students from other cultural backgrounds (e.g., Asian, Pacific Islander, American Indian/Alaska Native, and two or more races) make up the other 10%. In total, students of color now make up 52% of the public school population. The drastic change in student demographics demands that teacher education not conduct business as usual when preparing teacher educators.

Teachers face the challenge of supporting the educational needs of children from a myriad of ethnic and cultural backgrounds, and teacher education programs and teacher educators have the responsibility of preparing teachers to meet this challenge. To eliminate racial inequality and dismantle racism, it is imperative that we actively, collectively, and intentionally engage ourselves and teacher candidates in interrogating and disrupting inequitable social and educational policies and practices, combating racism at all levels, and ensuring equity and justice for all learners in K–12 and higher education. In addition, teacher education should address all forms of discrimination with our teacher candidates, paying particular attention to the intersectionality of race, gender, and concentrated poverty.

As a field, it is time to recognize that education has long been used as a tool to transmit the knowledge and values of the dominant culture while simultaneously serving as an indispensable mechanism for the social reproduction of racial inequality. Teacher education institutions are part of the education system that helps maintain and perpetuate such status quo (Picower & Kohli, 2017) and, as such, they carry the most responsibility in findings ways to solve this issue in teacher preparation programs.

BACKGROUND OF THIS BOOK

Founded in 1920, the Association of Teacher Educators (ATE) is the longest-standing national organization committed entirely to the improvement of teacher education. ATE "promotes advocacy, equity, leadership, and professionalism for teacher educators in all settings and supports quality education for all learners at all levels" (Association of Teacher Educators, 2021, para. 1). ATE's Diversity Committee is one of its standing committees and is charged with the responsibility of promoting, initiating, and coordinating diversity-related programs and initiatives in ATE. Over the last two years, the committee has been engaging in the process of reflecting and reenvisioning the possibilities of how teacher educators can better integrate antiracist education in our work with preservice and inservice teachers in our respective institutions and teacher education in general. To promote conversation and scholarship in this area, the committee sent out a call and invited teacher educators to engage in critical dialogues and reflections around theories, issues, complexities, and challenges of antiracist teacher education and to exchange critical ideas and theory/research-informed practices for preparing antiracist teachers. The editorial team received an overwhelming number of responses, indicating strong enthusiasm about this topic among our members and teacher educators around the nation.

The scope of this volume extends beyond existing scholarship on multicultural education and culturally responsive/sustaining pedagogy. It seeks to critically explore what antiracist teacher education is and what teacher education programs and teacher educators can do to prepare teacher candidates who are antiracists. While centering racism in our conversation, this volume also addresses the intersectionality of racism and other forms of social injustices that discriminate against people from various backgrounds.

This book is for teacher educators in various disciplinary areas and at all levels who want to join the cause to achieve racial and social justice. It is also intended for administrators and policymakers leading teacher education programs at national or state levels. It is an affinity space (Gee, 2004) for teacher educators to co-labor in the struggle, share and exchange ideas, and encourage each other in moving toward the goal of achieving racial and social justice in education.

ANTIRACIST EDUCATION AND ANTIRACIST TEACHER EDUCATION

Antiracism is a process of actively identifying and opposing racism in all its forms, whether intended or unintended. Sensoy and DiAngelo (2017a) define racism as

> White racial and cultural prejudice and discrimination, supported by institutional power and authority, used to the advantage of Whites and the disadvantage of people of color. Racism encompasses economic, political, social, and institutional actions and beliefs that perpetuate an unequal distribution of privileges, resources, and power between White people and peoples of color. (p. 125)

The goal of antiracism is to actively identify and challenge racist policies, behaviors, and beliefs that perpetuate racist ideas and actions at the individual, interpersonal, institutional, and structural levels. Many well-meaning educators believe simply being "not racist" is enough to eliminate inequality and racial discrimination. However, as Kendi (2019) observed, antiracism demands action. While terms like "not racist" see the problem of racism in individuals and groups, antiracism sees racial inequality as rooted in problems of power, policies, and institutional practices and emphasizes the importance of people taking actions to combat it (Kendi, 2019; Love, 2019). Antiracism also recognizes the intersectional and complex nature of identities. For example, a person may be assigned privilege based on one identity (e.g., class) and be discriminated against another (e.g., race). Thus, it is essential to center the analysis of race and racism through an intersectional lens (Sensoy & DiAngelo, 2017b).

This book is informed by a wide body of work and perspectives, including critical race theory (CRT; Bell, 1992; Delgado & Stepahncic, 2001; Dixson & Rousseau, 2006; Ladson-Billings & Tate, 2006; Matsuda et al., 1993) and Latinx critical theory (Solorzano & Delgado Bernal, 2001; Suzuki & Valencia, 1997; Valencia, 2010). These theories provide powerful tools for interrogating systemic inequality grounded in race, racism, and other forms of colonization, oppression, and subordination.

Ladson-Billings and Tate (2006) outlined the principles of CRT as it applies to education and the conceptual tools for advancing justice. The defining elements include the following: (a) race and racism are socially constructed; (b) racism is normal and common in the everyday experience of most POC; (c) interest convergence reveals the central function of White privilege in sustaining racial inequities (e.g., progress on civil rights is achieved only when the interest of POC intersects with White people; and (d) race must be viewed through intersectional and non-essentialist lenses, as systems of oppression operate in combination (race, sex, class, national origin, etc.) (Delgado & Stefancic, 2001).

Antiracist education explicitly critiques and challenges institutional racism by addressing the root causes of oppression in educational settings. The ultimate goal of antiracist education aims at dismantling all forms of discrimination and oppression (e.g., classism, sexism, heterosexism, ageism, monolingualism, nativism, ableism, etc.) in school policies, treatment of students from diverse backgrounds, curriculum, and instruction. Antiracist education is not a set of strategies, but an analytical framework that challenges educators to critically reflect on their beliefs and practices regarding racism in education and to take action to combat it.

Giroux (1988) posited teachers' beliefs or their ideologies offer powerful insight into teachers' practices. Cochran-Smith (2003) called on teacher educators to assume inquiry as a stance to investigate themselves and their own practices in addition to investigating students' constructions of race in the teacher education classroom and more broadly in teacher educators' experience. For example, Cochran-Smith examined her own work and her student teachers' constructions of race and was able to shed light on the complexities inherent in the teaching and examination of race in teacher education. In particular, she argued that teacher education that is antiracist rejects color-blind ideology, which is common among many educators, explicitly challenging them to ask hard questions, consider their own and their students' racial backgrounds, and think carefully about how race impacts learning opportunities. As Milner (2015) noted, "Teachers who adopt color-blind mind-sets and practices can lack the racial knowledge, sensitivity, and empathy necessary to successfully teach racially diverse students" (p. 17).

Antiracist teacher education prepares teacher candidates to become transformative intellectuals who are committed to understanding and engaging in equality and justice specific to the classrooms, schools, and the communities they serve (Giroux, 1988). It is within such contextually specific realms that such broader considerations of critical pedagogy regarding race, class, gender, democracy, justice, and oppression can begin to be taken up by teacher candidates in a meaningful and politically active light.

ORGANIZATION OF THE BOOK

The contributors to this volume are teacher educators who have passionately embarked on the difficult journey of antiracist teaching, research, clinical practice, and curriculum and program development. This book provides a theoretical background of antiracism in teacher education as well as evidence-based information to support the practices discussed. Chapter 1, "Grounding Antiracism and Guiding Educators Beginning with Self" by Nancy P. Gallavan, introduces the TABLETS Model (Thoughts, Actions, Beliefs, Language, Experiences, Traditions, and Settings). This model guides educators to think profoundly as reflective and reflexive practitioners to more fully understand themselves as antiracist educators and advocates of equity. Chapter 2, "Situating the Self in Context: Co-teaching to Prepare Antiracist Teachers to Teach in Urban Settings" by Laura Renzi and Matthew Kruger-Ross, details how to prepare antiracist STEM teachers. The authors share about the development of a master's program to prepare STEM teachers for urban contexts, utilizing antiracist pedagogies. Chapter 3, "L.I.S.T.E.N. Up: Antibias/Antiracist Orientations in Teacher Education" by Danné E. Davis and Sumi Hagiwara, discusses how to provide an antiracist orientation in teacher education classes. The authors reflect on their use of the orientation to advance racial justice and the challenges of engaging teacher education colleagues and students.

Chapter 4, "Diversity, Equity, and Inclusion Matter: Preparing Teacher Candidates to Become Activist Educators" by Benita R. Brooks, Ramona Pittman, Jaime Coyne, Tori Hollas, and Mae Lane, examines the experiences of teacher candidates who participated in a diversity, equity, and inclusion undergraduate certificate program. The theoretical underpinnings for this chapter focus on CRT and critical discourse analysis as a means to examine the experiences of teacher candidates. Chapter 5, "Making Space for Critical Thought amid State Prohibitions: Critical Race Theory as a Framework to Inform Course Design and Student Learning Objectives" by Marisol Diaz, Sarah M. Straub, Tonya Jeffery, and Brian Uriegas, describes how to reimagine the field experience for teacher preparation programs. A framework presents program and learning objectives and assignments using CRT perspectives.

Chapter 6, "Cross-Pollinating Teacher Preparation: Antiracist Inclusive Lesson Planning in Writers' Workshop" by Amy Tondreau, Laurie Rabinowitz, and Zachary Barnes, provides a roadmap for designing antiracist literacy curriculum and instruction, informed by Disabilities Studies and Critical Race Theory (DisCrit), Culturally Sustaining Pedagogy (CSP), and Universal Design for Learning (UDL). Chapter 7, "A Curriculum of Accomplicity: Foundations, Concepts, and Actions for Justice Work in Education" by Morna McDermott McNulty, unveils a curriculum that discusses what it means to be a White accomplice as opposed to a White ally. The author also considers how allyship has dominated the theoretical space in the field of antiracism. Last, Chapter 8, "Combating Anti-Asian Bias by Developing Intercultural Maturity through a Short-Term Study Abroad Program in China" by Ashley Lucas and Xiaoming Liu, demonstrates how real-world experiences provide instruction far beyond what can happen in the classroom.

This edited volume does not cover all the issues in antiracist teacher education. However, the authors of these chapters do provide a broad range of topics that we hope readers will find engaging, meaningful, and helpful for our journey together toward antiracist teacher education. The number of proposals submitted far exceeded the length allowances for this one book. Therefore, we have a second volume to continue the conversation and further expand the ways in which we can work on this critical topic.

We would like to end this introduction with a quote from Love (2019): "We must struggle together . . . to reimagine schools . . . based on the intersection of justice, antiracism, love, healing and joy" (p. 11). As teacher educators, we are called to take up the challenge to reimagine and transform teacher education for racial and social justice (Gorski, 2008; Ladson-Billings, 2014) and be part of the change for a better and more inclusive society that provides freedom, hope, opportunities, and justice for all, regardless of color, gender, class, and other social and cultural differences. It is in the spirit of love, hope, healing, and inclusion, we dedicate this book to teacher educators in our nation who are social justice-minded and work hard to create a better future for all learners.

REFERENCES

Bell, D. A. (1992). *Faces at the bottom of the well: The permanence of racism.* Perseus Book Group.

Cochran-Smith, M. (2003). Learning and unlearning: The education of teacher educators. *Teaching and Teacher Education, 19*(1), 5–28. https://doi.org/10.1016/S0742-051X(02)00091-4

Delgado, R., & Stefancic, J. (2001). *Critical race theory: An introduction*. NYU Press.

Dixson, A. D., & Rousseau, C. K. (2006). And we are not saved: Critical race theory in education ten years later. In A. D. Dixson & C. K. Rousseau (Eds.), *Critical race theory in education: All God's children got a song* (pp. 31–54). Routledge.

Gee, J. (2004). *Situated language and learning: A critique of traditional schooling*. Routledge.

Giroux, H. A. (1988). *Teachers as intellectuals: Toward a critical pedagogy of learning*. Bergin and Garvey.

Gorski, P. (2008). What we're teaching teachers: An analysis of multicultural teacher education coursework syllabi. *Teaching and Teacher Education, 25*(2), 309–318. https://doi.org/10.1016/j.tate.2008.07.008

Hussar, B., Zhang, J., Hein, S., Wang, K., Roberts, A., Cui, J., Smith, M., Bullock Mann, F., Barmer, A., & Dilig, R. (2020). *The condition of education 2020*. U.S. Department of Education. National Center for Education Statistics. https://nces.ed.gov/pubsearch/pubsinfo.asp?pubid=2020144

Kendi, I. X. (2019). *How to be an antiracist*. One World.

Ladson-Billings, G. (2014). Culturally relevant pedagogy 2.0: A.K.A. the remix. *Harvard Educational Review, 84*(1), 74–84. https://doi.org/10.17763/haer.84.1.p2rj131485484751

Ladson-Billings, G., & Tate, W. F., IV. (2006). Critical race theory of education. In A. D. Dixson & C. K. Rousseau (Eds.), *Critical race theory in education: All God's children got a song* (pp. 31–54). Routledge.

Love, B. L. (2019). *We want to do more than survive: Abolitionist teaching and the pursuit of educational freedom*. Beacon Press.

Matsuda, M., Lawrence, C., Delgado, R., & Crenshaw, K. (1993). *Words that wound: Critical race theory, assaultive speech, and the First Amendment*. Worldview.

Milner, H. R. (2015). *Understanding diversity, opportunity gaps, and teaching in today's classroom*. Harvard University Press.

Picower, B., & Kohli, R. (Eds.). (2017). *Confronting racism in teacher education: Counternarratives of critical practice*. Routledge.

Sensoy, O., & DiAngelo, R. (2017a). *Is everyone really equal? An introduction to key concepts in social justice education*. Teachers College Press.

Sensoy, O., & DiAngelo, R. (2017b). "We are all for diversity, but . . ." How faculty hiring committees reproduced whiteness and practical suggestions for how they can change. *Harvard Educational Review, 87*(4), 557–580. https://doi.org/10.17763/1943-5045-87.4.557

Solorzano, D. G., & Delgado Bernal, D. (2001). Examining transformational resistance through critical race theory and LatCrit framework: Chicana and Chicano students in an urban context. *Urban Education, 36*(3), 308–342. https://doi.org/10.1177/0042085901363002

Suzuki, L. A., & Valencia, R. R. (1997). Race-ethnicity and measured intelligence: Educational implications. *American Psychologist, 52*(10), 1103–1112.

Valencia, R. R. (2010). *Dismantling contemporary deficit thinking: Educational thought and practice*. Routledge.

Chapter 1

Grounding Antiracism and Guiding Educators Beginning with Self

Nancy P. Gallavan

Every educator is accountable for creating meaningful learning environments and building mindful community relationships where all participants feel safe, welcome, and wanted. These processes rely on and resonate with essential factors for being accepted, becoming fulfilled, and belonging wholeheartedly. Engaging in and ensuring diversity, inclusion, equity, and social justice in ways that are authentic, profound, and dynamic are integral to establishing this comfortable sense of place. To guide and support educators—prekindergarten through higher education—in their growth, development, and transformation, this chapter grounds antiracism based on the researcher's TABLETS Model. Each component of the TABLETS Model (Thoughts, Actions, Beliefs, Language, Experiences, Traditions, and Settings) contributes significantly to every educator's natural and holistic existence personally, professionally, and pedagogically. Delving into reflectivity and discerning through reflexivity equip and empower educators to understand themselves more fully, honestly, and consciously. Educators strengthen their sense of efficacy and agency as they transform the teaching, learning, and schooling for all participants, beginning with themselves.

INTRODUCTION

Every educator is, first and foremost, a person who was born into a family, raised in a community, and prepared to serve in a profession; likewise, every educator currently has a family, lives in a community, and serves in a profession in ways that may or may not resemble the educator's life in the past or the educator's life in the future. The words *family*, *community*, and *profession* may be considered common references, accepted ideas, and universal concepts that infer the same meanings for and messages about all people across time, space, and matter. However, each of these three words conveys a social construct created by humans, not by nature; connected to many different factors created by humans, not by nature; prioritized by humans, again, not by nature.

Social constructs tend to be defined by the socially dominant and, frequently, self-determined group of people who may alter the definitions with or without recognition of and/or respect for diverse populations, multicultural perspectives, and social justice. Consequently, the definitions of social constructs tend to be regulated, reinforced, and, most significantly, revised, through spoken conversations, written texts, and aired/posted media frequently, without question or concern of their influence and their impact.

Notably, social constructs tend to be associated with distinguishing policies and distinctive parameters that shape institutional structures, systems, and standards found across society, for example, civic, corporate, financial, educational, governmental, medical, recreational, religious, and residential. Foundational policies and framed parameters are deliberately designed, developed, and defended to include, promote, and empower selected portions of the population. Concomitantly, particular policies and parameters tend to exclude, marginalize, and disempower selected portions of the population identified primarily by cultural characteristics including, but not limited to, race, ethnicity, gender, religion, economics, language, age, and so forth. Given their genesis and evolution, social constructs often result in biased, prejudicial, and discriminatory stereotypes applied ubiquitously, knowingly and unknowingly, across humanity.

Specifically, the social constructs of *family*, *community*, and *profession* incorporate unlimited portrayals illustrative and inclusive of every person from the past and the present, portrayals that will continue to evolve and expand into the future. Too often in schools and classrooms, the learners, and the learner's families, communities, and communities' professionals are omitted from the portraits depicting the people who are valued and visualized in the comprehensive mural, frequently referred to as the "big picture," of the United States.

To wit, most parts of educational curriculum, instruction, assessment, and community tend to be directed by and delimited to the dissemination of heritage, rather than history. The regurgitation of heritage preserves and propagates the events of the past and present selected by only a few decision-makers. The powerful posturing of the socially dominant group to defend a heritage that excludes many people, especially Black, Indigenous, and People of Color, from learning about their own history concomitantly prevents everyone from learning about everyone's history (Wallace-Wells, 2021). These defiant efforts are exemplified by ongoing controversial discussions and contentious debates relevant to critical race theory (Crenshaw et al., 1996) and the 1919 Project (Hannah-Jones, 2019). Living in an isolated, fictitious conception of the present and denying the amalgamated factual composition of the past and present negate the rich diversity of families, communities, and professionals from participating equitably in and contributing rightfully to the present and future. Consequently, every learner is denied "information, access, and opportunity" (Gallavan in Wink & Putney, 2002, p. 158) to understand, appreciate, flourish, share, and preserve the complete story of everyone's cultural journals and characteristic joys throughout their lives.

Educators have formed their cultural knowledge, skills, and dispositions on their self-selected assortment of individual values situated within the array of institutional visions that the educator acknowledges and accepts. Generally viewed as well-informed, kindhearted, authority figures, educators tend to move through their worlds (Webster, 2021) consciously and unconsciously replicating the practices from their past into the present and the future to fulfill their presumed purposes. Most likely, their practices and purposes relate to and focus on the socially dominant group of people while their practices and purposes may not relate to or focus on any or all nondominant groups of people determined by chance and by choice. This "generational perpetuation of practice" (Gallavan, 2007, p. 17) contributes significantly to both protecting educators from individual responsibility and ownership of their efficacy and agency while projecting the escalation of institutional domination and lifelong regulation.

Although most educators are prepared as reflective practitioners, few educators engage in extensive reflection consistently that reaps meaningful modifications in their practices associated with cultural competence and social justice (Solorzano & Bernal, 2001). Moreover, fewer educators are prepared as reflexive practitioners who embark on an intensive understanding of the complex intersectionality of their values and expectations with their visions and expressions that yield mindful transformation in their purposes. Accountability connotes that every educator needs to assess their awareness, that is, their conscientization (Freire, 1972), associated with what they do *and* with who they are. Their practices and purposes must ensure cultural humility, curriculum development, instructional strategies, assessment techniques, classroom interactions, and differentiating learning so every learner experiences optimal motivation, engagement, curiosity, connections, creativity, and achievement.

This chapter introduces the author's TABLETS Model; TABLETS stands for Thoughts, Actions, Beliefs, Language, Experiences, Traditions, and Settings. These seven components guide and support educators, prekindergarten through higher education, teachers, and administrators through their transformative journeys as reflective and reflexive practitioners in order to ensure equity in education for all learners. Understandingly, the TABLETS Model applies across all biased, prejudicial, and discriminatory stereotypes; however, this chapter is contextualized in the presence and power of racism and antiracism.

ANTIRACISM

In 2019, Kendi wrote, "Racist: one who is supporting a racist policy through their actions or inaction or expressing a racist idea" (p. 13). "Antiracist: one who is supporting an antiracist policy through their actions or interaction or expressing antiracist ideas" (p. 9). For many educators, these two definitions convey clearly delineated binary positions, that is, direct opposites comprising distinct orientations describing their positionality related to the social construct of race. In the United States, the construct of race embodies far more than the identification of skin color, physical traits, and common ancestry of non-White identity. The construct of race encapsulates the irrational devaluing and dehumanizing, the zone of nonbeing (Fanon, 1952, p. 10) forcing Black, Indigenous, and People of Color to exist in a lived contradiction (Gordon, 2005). Throughout the history of this country, individuals and institutions have proliferated their construct of race as acts of racism communicating inferiorization and antipathy (Blum, 2002) with blatantly aggressive bigotry, denigration, hatred, and violence.

The politicized racialization of people based on race, specifically Black, Indigenous, and People of Color, results in singling people out by segregating them for unique and unwanted treatment. Occurring at both the macro and micro levels of society, racialization leverages racism categorically and systemically. Wilkerson (2020) details in her book *Caste: The Origins of Our Discontents* that race and racism are a form of caste, the calculated, condescending, and callous social stratification that divides people and denies them equality, renouncing the frequently repeated oath of "liberty and justice for all" (United States of America, Pledge of Allegiance, 1892).

Racism and antiracism comprise evolutionary constructs with many different, ever-changing meanings and messages determined by individuals and institutions. The meanings and messages associated with racism and antiracism continue to change to meet the needs, interests, and, most importantly, benefits of individuals and institutions based on a vast array of explanations and justifications. Educators may find conversations confusing and controversial as they grapple with their predispositions and propensities. Davis (n.d., para 2) reminds us, "In a racist society, it is not enough to be non-racist; we must be anti-racist." Therefore, as educators self-interpret, they self-identify with the nuanced concepts and characteristics of racism and antiracism in their own ways.

Kendi's (2019) two definitions may suggest primary points distantly placed away from one another on a never-ending straight-line continuum as described in this quote from DiAngelo.

> Our identities are not separate from the White supremacist society in which we are raised. And our patterns of cross-racial engagement are not merely a function of our unique personalities. . . . Wherever we may be on the continuum of seeing and addressing racism, we are not at the end. (DiAngelo, 2021, p. vii)

Therefore, most likely to avoid isolating themselves as one of these preconceived extremes, educators tend to insert their own intermediary points on the continuum attributed to the infinite nuances of racism and antiracism accounting for themselves and sometimes about the people around them, both near and far. These intermediary points denote each educator's own impressions of growth, development, and transformation, especially in relation to the factors impacting and influencing the many facets of and contexts related to their personal, professional, and pedagogical journeys.

Continuum as a Graphic Representation

Images of a continuum are not limited to straight lines (a line extending in two directions) or rays (a line extending in only one direction). A continuum can be displayed as a curved line or ray, circle, spiral, set of steps, blocks of categories, shape, and network, among various designs. As educators invest time and energy into learning, thinking, and understanding antiracism, the initial image of the selected continuum most likely will change to accommodate their discoveries. The complexities involved in constructing a graphic representation may transition with the investigation and acquisition of new data (qualitative and/or quantitative), information (data analysis), and knowledge (information application) that contribute to our wisdom (contextualized expertise). Plus, constructing a graphic representation associated with antiracism allows educators to connect verbal and visual learning efficiently and effectively. Importantly, graphic representations provide avenues to document ideas through the use of symbols or drawings by eliminating cultural, educational, language, literacy, and experiential barriers.

For this research, the continuum of educator growth, development, and transformations, particularly associated with antiracism, is shown in figure 1.1. Further, figure 1.1 represents this continuum as an ever-expanding and contracting, continually turning and moving borderless space of

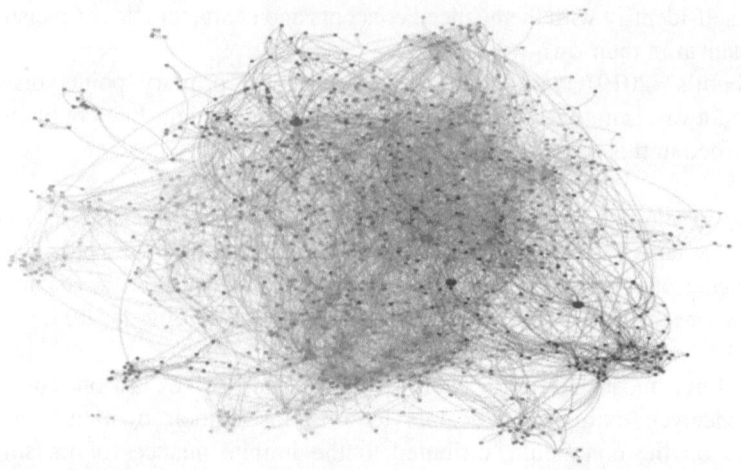

Figure 1.1 Gallavan's Cloud of Growth, Development, and Transformation. (Image used by A. Kruseman, n.d.)

interconnecting and intersecting lines with various sizes of points on some of the lines. Later in this chapter, this continuum, now called Gallavan's Cloud of Growth, Development, and Transformation, is applied to the TABLETS Model.

Noticing and Noting Racism

Racism encompasses "the marginalization and/or oppression of People of Color based on a social constructed racial hierarchy that privileges White people" (Anti-Defamation League [ADL], 2020, Racism section, para. 1). The ADL describes race as the category in which society places people based on their biology created for social and political reasons. The ADL categorizes systemic racism as the combination of systems, institutions, and factors that advantage White people and both disadvantage and cause harm and violence to Black, Indigenous, and People of Color. The ADL states that systemic racism (a) is grounded in the history of our laws and institutions which were created on the foundation of White supremacy, (b) exists in the institutions and policies that advantage White people and disadvantage Black, Indigenous, and People of Color, and (c) takes place in interpersonal communication and behavior that maintains and supports systemic inequities and systemic racism (ADL, 2020).

All educators have been subjected to and segregated by race, racism, and systemic racism. Although the U.S. Supreme Court declared in 1954 that racial segregation in public schools violated the equal protection clause of the Fourteenth Amendment (Justia, n.d.), everyone involved in schooling enacted laws, established policies, and embraced behaviors to circumvent the Supreme Court ruling. The laws, policies, and behaviors perpetuated the visions of individuals and the values of institutions. Supreme Court Justice Thurgood Marshall, who presented the Brown family in 1954, later stated:

> I wish I could say that racism and prejudice were only distant memories. We must dissent from the indifference. We must dissent from the apathy. We must dissent from the fear, the hatred, and the mistrust. . . . We must dissent because American can do better because American has no choice but to do better. (Marshall, 1992, para. 12)

Consistently since the founding of this country, laws, policies, and behaviors adopted to protect and promote the socially dominant group of people have been avoided and altered. Laws, policies, and behaviors that may have been shared openly and conducted overtly have been avoided and altered to be secreted clandestinely and conducted covertly. As educators sustained the presence and power of heritage rather than history across their practices, educators contributed to systemic racism. Beginning in the 1600s, racism via the deficit model has been pervasively applied in prekindergarten through higher education schools and classrooms (Valencia, 2010). Academic and social failures assigned to learners are accounted to predetermined alleged deficit factors, such as home issues, at-risk conditions, unpreparedness, low economic status, and community expectations. Hiring and retaining failures assigned to educators are accounted to predetermined alleged deficit factors, such as few qualified applicants, inability to communicate clearly with learners, cultural misalignment with learners and their families, anticipated isolation as the only non-White teacher, and so forth (Ash et al., 2020). Rather than addressing the causes, educators tend to address the effects of racism and systemic racism.

Educator racism occurs directly and indirectly, explicitly and implicitly, intentionally and unintentionally, consciously and unconsciously, and all the multifarious nuances associated with and around each of these extremes. Too often, decisions made by educators include microaggressions and macroaggressions manifested as negative, derogatory, and hostile insults; invalidations; and assaults that influence us positively and impact us negatively. Webster (2021) clarifies that influences are outcomes that change a person in an indirect, yet important way, while impacts are outcomes that change a person in a direct, forceful way. Microaggressions and macroaggressions not only influence and impact the recipient and people who are culturally aligned with the recipient, microaggressions and macroaggressions influence and impact everyone. History verifies that the impacts of racism and systemic racism resonate through space, time, and matter.

To address racism, educators must become conditioned to noticing and noting racism perpetuated by the institutional structures and their individual selves. Shah and Coles (2020) proffer a theoretical framework of racial noticing extending the research on teaching noticing. Racial noticing involves the three processes for noting and embedding across the teaching, learning, and schooling: (a) attending to racial phenomenon, that is, identity in relation to their positionality and privilege; racial disparities and implicit bias evident in formal and informal interactions; and representation in curriculum, courses, extracurricular activities, and conflict management; (b) interpreting racial phenomena, that is, recognition of racial incidents; identification of racial narratives; and rationalization of racial discrimination; and (c) responding to racial phenomena, that is, engagement in dialogue (internal and external); modification of practices through reflection. When educators notice and note racism, they are more likely to account honestly and holistically for the contextual influences and impacts that perpetuate racism.

Often, individual educators claim that they are not racist and that their institutions are free of systemic racism. However, educators, individually and institutionally, would benefit from delving into their practices and purposes for evidence. All educators rely upon their beliefs that sustain their behaviors. Many educators' beliefs and accompanying behaviors are based on benchmarks and may be biased. Similarly, all educators rely upon truthful, trustworthy, and transparent data for their decisions. Decisions morph into delivery and possibly discrimination. When educators are biased and discriminatory in their words, actions, and interactions, they are denying a sense of *being, that is, living and learning now*, for all their learners.

All educators rely upon the patterns for planning. Patterns tend to morph into presumptions, and presumptions may reveal prejudices. When educators are prejudicial, they are denying a sense of *becoming, living and learning in the near future*, for all of their learners. Likewise, all educators rely upon standards and systems, many of which are steeped in statistics. Statistics relate to standards, systems, and structures that impact strategies with potential stereotypes. When educators stereotype, they are denying a sense of *belonging, living and learning forever, everywhere, and with everyone*. Educators must practice critical consciousness to ensure being, becoming, and belonging for everyone, including themselves as presented in table 1.1.

Antiracism as Critical Consciousness

Critical consciousness embodies the "ability to recognize and analyze systems of inequality and the commitment to take action against these systems" (Watts et al., 1999, pp. 255–256). Three components of critical consciousness include "information, access, and opportunity" (Gallavan in Wink & Putney,

Table 1.1 Evidentiary Evolution of Educator Racism

Internal Mechanisms	External Maintenance	Educator Manifestations	Unwanted Materializations
Beliefs	Behaviors	Benchmarks	Biases
Data	Decisions	Delivery	Discrimination
Patterns	Planning	Presumptions	Prejudices
Statistics	Standards/Systems	Strategies	Stereotypes

2002, p. 158) as shown in figure 1.2. Everyone needs information incorporating narrative and numerical data to acknowledge and understand, that is, *to know* people, places, and perspectives. Everyone needs access offering liberatory and equitable abilities to enter and proceed, that is, to go places and be in spaces physically, cognitively, affectively, socially, imaginatively, financially, electronically, and so forth. Everyone needs opportunities and openness extending choices, chances, and channels, that is, *to do* what everyone can do. Everyone wants to gain information, access, and opportunities in order to experience life to its fullest. Likewise, everyone possesses both the responsibility and the ownership to give information, access, and opportunities to people around them, near and far. The reciprocity exchanged between gaining and giving exists for all people throughout life.

In the center of figure 1.2, where the three spheres overlap, is the inner space filled by the responsible owner of critical consciousness. Educators fill this inner space for and with their learners. Educators need to ensure equitable information, access, and opportunity for every learner and without bias, prejudice, discrimination, and stereotypes.

Within this inner space, educators grow, develop, and transform by grappling with the tensions associated with gaining and giving; the paradoxes associated with who gains, the reasons that gain, and the amounts they gain; and the uncertainties associated with choices and chances and channels. As decision-makers,

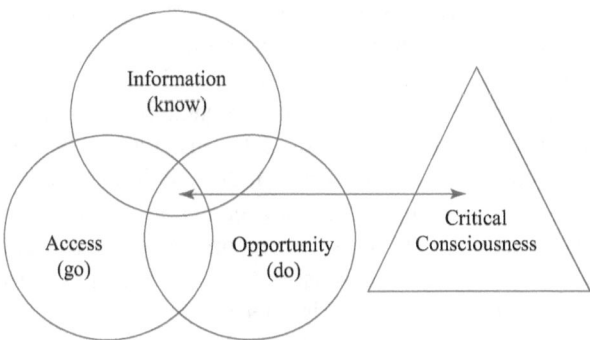

Figure 1.2 Critical Consciousness. (Gallavan in Wink & Putney, 2002)

educators serve as gatekeepers regulating all facets of teaching, learning, and schooling. For example, educators make choices as to which learners are taught what information via their curriculum, instruction, and assessments. Also, educators provide channels as to which learners receive what access to particular programs and reserved resources and offer learners with chances with opportunities to participate in special activities and extracurricular events.

Reflectivity, Reflexivity, and Refractivity

As educators self-assess their practices, they tend to engage in reflection, the process of thinking about educational situations. Schön (1983, 1987) describes two types of reflection: in-action and on-action. Reflectivity in-action occurs when an educator realizes that changes need to be made immediately, that is, at the moment as teaching, learning, and schooling are happening. When reflecting in-action, educators respond spontaneously by being present and perceptive to the learners as individuals and members of a group interacting with the curriculum, instruction, assessment, and community. Reflectivity on-action occurs when an educator recognizes that modifications need to be made after the teaching, learning, and schooling have happened.

Educator reflexivity tends to focus primarily on the educators' practices, that is, what they do in order and who they are in order for their learners to improve what they do and who they are. By reflecting on and modifying their practices, both in-action and on-action, educators can enhance their sense of self-efficacy (Bandura, 1997) empowering them to produce targeted outcomes. Reflection aligns well with educators' standards and overarching expectations, that is, their responsibilities to increase learner attendance, achievement, and completion of a grade, course, program, and so forth.

Educators' external meaningful actions are intertwined with educators' internal mindful consciousness. Through reflexivity, educators focus on who they are by thinking about their thoughts and feelings generated by their actions, language, experiences, traditions, and settings. Reflexive educators consider their internal capabilities that fortify their external capacities. Through reflexivity, educators uncover and understand their individual identities and cultural characteristics, clearly and comprehensively transforming their sense of efficacy and agency (Bandura, 2001). Bandura (2001) explains that human agency, characterized by forethought and intentionality, engenders self-regulation and ownership prompting educators to become responsible producers of social interaction. As educators increase awareness of their purposes, both sensibilities and sensitivities play significant roles in their decision-making with and for every learner holistically.

Educators engage in reflectivity and reflexivity on their past and present by contemplating what they do, coupled with who they are. Educators must also consider their future by planning what they want to do coupled with who they want to be. Moving from retrospection to prospection involves the process of authentic, profound, and dynamic introduction to ensure equity across education via antiracist purposes and practices. This transformative journey tends to involve complex, confusing, and confrontative insights as educators attempt to connect, disconnect, and reconnect their thoughts, actions, and beliefs. Transitioning from retrospection to prospection conjoins intellectual perceptions with socialized discernments of learned and lived experiences. Mitchell (2016) refers to this inner space as *perezhivanie* from the research of Vygotsky (1935), describing it as a prism with three attributes. The three attributes include: (a) the mediating role between the person and the environment, that is, growth; (b) the strengthening consciousness of the person and practice (what I do), that is, development; and (c) the interpretive properties of the person and the purpose (who I am), that is, transformation, as shown in figure 1.3.

When light enters the prism as a single straight stream of white, the light slows down and is split into many streams of colors as seen in a rainbow. As the colors exit the prism the light regains its speed as it spreads more broadly. For educators, the prismatic refractivity associated with antiracism bends, separates, and slows the input, that is, the biased, discriminatory, prejudicial stereotypes of hate and violence into different angles producing output that enables and empowers educators to transform their practices and purposes. And, like the refractive properties that reflect the light internally into many different facets, educators begin their transformative journeys with wisdom from multiple perspectives because "ultimately we teach who we are" (Palmer, 2007, pp. 2–3).

Discomfort

Engaging in reflectivity, reflexivity, and refractivity related to educators' practices and purposes prompts educators to acknowledge and actuate both their capabilities and capacities. Capabilities include knowledge, skills, and dispositions that educators have learned (by choice, chance, and channels). Capacities identify the knowledge, skills, and dispositions that educators can

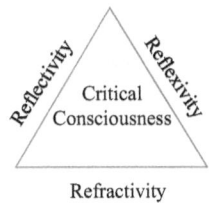

Figure 1.3 Inner Space of Critical Consciousness.

and may learn with modeling, guidance, and support. Capability relates to expressed performance, that is, the educator's way and proficiency to fulfill expectations; capacity relates to extended possibilities, that is, the educator's will and potential to exceed expectations. Engaging in reflection and reflexivity begins with capability and builds on capacity.

Revisiting figure 1.2 illustrating critical consciousness, capability means the educator stays safely ensconced within the self-determined inner space. Capacity means the educator suspends the perceived edges and expands the inner space by moving intentionally through blurred boundaries and unbundled boxes relevant to their personal, professional, and pedagogical existence. Educators are invited to listen intuitively to their inner spaces with courage where compassionate, connective, and creative energy is generated (Palmer, 1997).

When educators assess their practices and purposes in ways that are authentic, profound, and dynamic, most likely they will encounter discomfort as they disrupt, dismantle, and demystify the acknowledged and unacknowledged presence and power of racism and systemic racism that permeate all parts of their lives. Prior to initiating the complexities and ambiguities associated with critical self-assessment, educators are encouraged to adopt a multifaceted approach and attitudes of flexibility (Boler, 1999). Applying the pedagogy of discomfort (Boler, 1999), educators must leave their comfort zones in order to analyze their critical consciousness, experiencing cognitive distortions, emotional dissonance, and social distancing as they explore the moral dimensions or intersectionality of what they do and who they are. See figure 1.4 Critical Conciousness (Gallavan in Wink & Putney, 2002). Boler (1999) details this process as often accompanied by feelings of guilt, accusation, defensiveness, fear, and anger. Specifically, anger may occur as (a) moral anger, that is, resentment toward the unjustifiable accusation; and as (b) defensive anger, that is, perceived fear of loss and change especially related to personal identity, especially through exposure to and expressions of vulnerability.

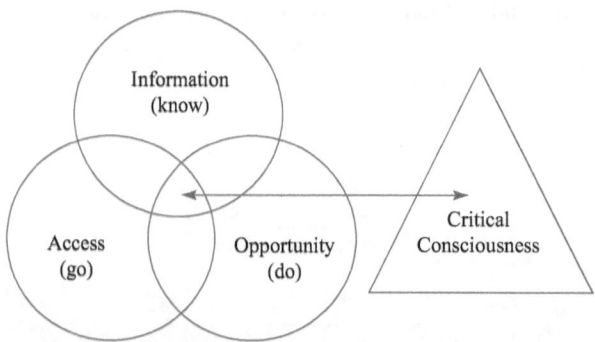

Figure 1.4 Critical Consciousness. (Gallavan in Wink & Putney, 2002)

Brené Brown (2012) defines vulnerability as requisite throughout the quest for wholeheartedness. This quest involves creating a brave space encouraging honesty, intentionality, and gratitude. Being vulnerable incorporates (a) courage to embrace uncertainty, take risks, and experience emotional exposure; (b) connections to energize, begin, and end relationships; and (c) compassion to empathize with ourselves and the people around us, near and far (Brown, 2012).

Being vulnerable requires educators to adopt the courage to be a conscious educator, the connections to become the educator they want to be, and compassion to belong to the community of conscious educators. However, as educators progress with their critical self-assessment, they encounter an internal struggle as they acknowledge that racism and systemic racism are substantial, sustained, subtle, and subversive.

THE TABLETS MODEL

The TABLETS Model offers educators a guide to engage in an honest and intentional self-assessment of their knowledge, skills, and dispositions influencing their practices and purposes evident in the teaching, learning, and schooling. Vital to their readiness, receptiveness, and responsiveness (Gallavan & Merritt, 2018), educators benefit by establishing a brave space, expanding their capacities associated with the inner space of critical consciousness, and, yes, experiencing vulnerability. The TABLETS Model identifies seven components related to every part of an educator's life, that is, inclusive of time, space, and matter. And, similar to an electronic device, the TABLETS Model provides a mechanism to record data, information, knowledge, and wisdom in a graphic representation. Through reflection and reflexivity (and the inner space of refraction), educators can acknowledge and actuate themselves personally, professionally, and pedagogically on their continuum of antiracism.

TABLETS is an acronym for the seven components—Thoughts, Actions, Beliefs, Language, Experiences, Traditions, and Settings—displayed on this continuum called a cloud (previously introduced in this chapter). Gallavan's Cloud of Growth, Development, and Transformation includes many interconnecting and intersecting lines punctuated by points. Each of the positioned points represents a letter in the TABLETS Model and contributes to the overall model. However, the shapes and sizes of the points vary with the educator's current emphasis and focus associated with each of the components. In figure 1.5, Thoughts, Actions, and Beliefs are emphasized with language featured in the center in the quest for critical consciousness and wholeheartedness. However, Experiences, Traditions, and Settings contribute substantially to growth, development, and transformation. Every educator's cloud will graphically represent the seven components of TABLETS Model differently depending on the educator's processes with reflection and reflexivity. See figure 1.5 Gallavan's Cloud of Growth, Development, and Transformation as an example.

The components of Thoughts, Actions, and Beliefs correspond, respectively, to cognitive, physical, and social/emotional functions. The component of Language corresponds to written and/or spoken language at all registers of communication that is expressed and enjoyed when listening and/or viewing. The component of Experiences corresponds to encounters and events. The component of Traditions corresponds to customs, rituals, habits, preferences, and so forth. And, the component of Settings corresponds to places, locations, areas, and so forth, including physical and cultural geographic scenarios and assumptions about settings.

Each of the seven components should be contextualized in seven ways: (a) Era—from the past and/or present; (b) Direction—as generated and/or as received and/or witnessed; and (c) Goal—as intentional and/or unintentional. Continuing, contextualization applicable to the seven components includes: (d) Impetus—as an individual value and/or as an institutional vision; (e) Loci—as an authority and/or as a peer; (f) Number—as an isolated component and/or as the intersection of components; and (g) Sequence—as an isolated event and/or continuous events. Examining each facet of contextualization reveals the choices, chances, and channels that have positively influenced and negatively impacted the educator throughout their lives.

The process of grounding antiracism on the TABLETS Model invites educators to self-assess via reflection (what I do and what I want to do) and reflexivity (who I am and who I want to be) as a critical conscious educator.

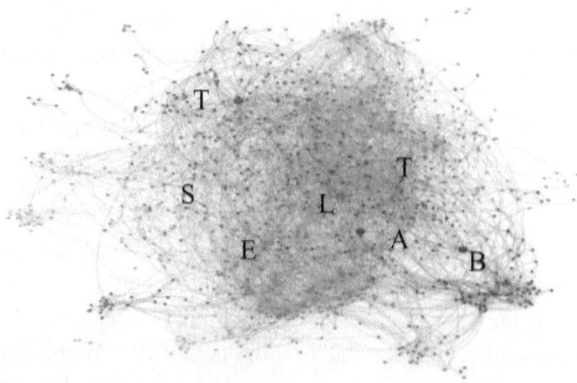

Figure 1.5 Gallavan's Cloud of Growth, Development, and Transformation. (imaged used by A. Kruseman, n.d.)

Descriptions of each component and corresponding prompts for self-assessment are presented in Table 1.2.

Five overarching conditions must guide educators engaged in honest self-assessment of the TABLETS Model: (a) Are they true? (b) Are they fair? (c) Are they kind? (d) Are they helpful? and (e) Are they necessary? Three additional overarching conditions apply to Experiences, Traditions, and Settings: (f) What occurred for you and everyone involved directly and indirectly? (g)

Table 1.2 TABLETS Model Component Descriptions and Self-Assessment Prompts

Components	Self-Assessment Prompts
Thoughts	What are my thoughts about racism and about antiracism?
	How and why do I possess my thoughts about racism and about antiracism?
Actions	What are my actions about racism and about antiracism?
	How and why do I demonstrate my actions about racism and about antiracism?
Beliefs	What are my beliefs about racism and about antiracism?
	How and why do I possess my beliefs about racism and about antiracism?
Language	What are my words about racism and about antiracism?
	How and why do I say/write my words about racism and about antiracism?
	What words about racism and about antiracism do I listen to and view?
	How and why do I listen to and view these words about racism and about antiracism?
	How and why do my words influence, impact, and affect my interactions with people around me—near and far?
Experiences	What are my experiences with racism and with antiracism?
	How and why do my experiences with racism and with antiracism influence, impact, and affect me?
	How and why do my traditions with racism and with antiracism influence, impact, and affect my interactions with people around me—near and far?
Traditions	What are my traditions associated with racism and with antiracism?
	How and why do my traditions influence, impact, and affect me?
	How and why do my traditions associated with racism and with antiracism influence, impact, and affect my interactions with people around me—near and far?
Settings	What are my assumptions about settings associated with racism and with antiracism?
	How and why do my assumptions about settings associated with racism and with antiracism influence, impact, and affect me?
	How and why do my assumptions about settings associated with racism and with antiracism influence, impact, and affect my interactions with people around me—near and far?

How did the events that occurred influence and/or impact you and everyone involved directly and indirectly? and (h) Why are the influences and impacts important to self-assess?

A seventh grade middle school teacher shares a self-assessment contextualized in racism and antiracism highlighting the seven components of the TABLETS Model: *Every day I hear the statements and read information related to racism and antiracism, especially the words spoken by my students and their families. Their **language** is clear and concerning. And every day I discover more details of U.S. history inclusive of all people. My **thoughts** now center on differentiating between fact and fiction, which, in turn, fuel my **actions**. I have strengthened my advocacy and allyship as an antiracist by joining groups for online dialogue that have led directly to the words and actions I use in my classroom and the faculty room. With focused thoughts and refortified energy, some of the past beliefs fueled by my family, friends, teachers, and community have been completely extinguished and new **beliefs** have been sparked. I am listening closely to antiracist leaders and acquiring new language that is more intentional and inclusive. I realize that the wildfire is no longer burning until I visit some of my family and friends; then I mentally revisit past **experiences** and **traditions**, question their effects on my current positionality, especially with my seventh-grade students, who I want to become advocates and allies for everyone, especially themselves.*

CONCLUSION

"Antiracism is the commitment to fight racism wherever you find it, including in yourself. It's the only way forward." This statement by Ijeoma Oluo (n.d., para 1) encapsulates this chapter invested in grounding antiracism with the TABLETS Model. The TABLETS Model identifies seven components that must be considered as seven essential markers on every educator's continuum of learning and living that guide and support their growth, development, and transformation. Through reflectivity, reflexivity, and refractivity, educators engender trust, hope, strength, and courage in themselves, their learners, their learners' families, and their communities blurring the boundaries and unbundling the boxes within and away from their educational environments.

Educators are encouraged to place their TABLETS so they receive the single stream of white light that slows, separates, and bends the input to project an angled output comprising seven broad bands of colorful light. Educators can acknowledge their positive diverse identities; dignify and respect the diverse identities of everyone around them—near and far; vary their curriculum, instruction, assessments, and community so all learners learn about themselves and everyone around them throughout time; adopt the processes of reflectivity, reflexivity, and refractivity as an antiracist educator; notice the presence and power of racism, systemic racism, and antiracism as both influencing and impacting their practices and purposes; and exercise grace and gratitude.

REFERENCES

Anti-Defamation League (ADL). (2020). *Racism.* https://www.adl.org/racism

Ash, A. N., Hill, R., Risdon, S. N., & Jun, A. (2020). Anti-racism in higher education: A model for change. *Race and Pedagogy Journal, 4*(3), 1–35. https://soundideas.pugetsound.edu/rpj/vol4/iss3/2

Bandura, A. (1997). *Self-efficacy: The exercise of control.* W. H. Freeman.

Bandura, A. (2001). Social cognitive theory: An agentic perspective. *Annual Review of Psychology, 52*, 1–26. https://doi.org/10.1146/annurev.psych.52.1.1

Blum, L. (2002). *I'm not a racist, But . . . the moral quandary of race.* Cornell University Press.

Boler, M. (1999). *Feeling power: Emotions and education.* Routledge.

Brown, B. (2012). *Daring greatly: How the courage to be vulnerable transform the way we live, love, parent, and lead.* Penguin.

Brown, B. (2011, January 3). The power of vulnerability. [Ted Talk]. https://www.youtube.com/watch?v=iCvmsMzlF7o

Crenshaw, K., Gotanda, N., Peiler, G., & Thomas, K. (Eds.). (1996). *Critical race theory: The key writing that formed the movement.* The New Press.

Davis, A. Y. (n.d.). *Anti-racism and criminal justice reform resources.* University of California-Santa Cruz; Institute for Social Transformation. https://transform.ucsc.edu/anti-racism-resources/

DiAngelo, R. (2021). *Nice racism: How progressive White people perpetuate racial harm.* Beacon Press.

Fanon, F. (1952). *Black skin, white masks.* Grove Press.

Freire, P. (1972). *Cultural action for freedom.* Penguin.

Gallavan, N. P. (2002). Cultural competency and critical consciousness for transformative education. In J. Wink & L. G. Putney (Eds.), *Visions of Vygotsky* (pp. 157–175). Allyn and Bacon.

Gallavan, N. P. (2007). Seven perceptions influencing novice teachers' efficacy and cultural competence. *Journal of Praxis in Multicultural Education, 2*(1), 5–19. https://digitalscholarship.unlv.edu/cgi/viewcontent.cgi?article=1020&context=jpme

Gallavan, N. P., & Merritt, J. P. (2018). Reinforcing MAT course goals during internship experiences via Gallavan's seven essential elements. In N. P. Author & L. G. Putney (Eds.), *ATE Yearbook XXVI: Building upon inspirations and inspirations with hope, courage, and strength: Teacher educators' commitment to today's teachers and tomorrow's leaders* (pp. 43–62). Rowman & Littlefield.

Gordon, L. R. (2005). Through the zone of nonbeing: A reading of *Black Skin, White Masks* in celebration of Fanon's eightieth birthday. *CLR James Journal, 11*(1), 1–43.

Hannah-Jones, N. (2019). *The 1619 Project: The new origin story.* One World.

Justia. (n.d.). Brown v. Board of Education of Topeka, 347 U.S. 483 (1954). https://supreme.justia.com/cases/federal/us/347/483/

Kendi, I. X. (2019). *How to be an antiracist*. Random House.

Kruseman, A. (n.d.). *Social network analysis on tweets*. https://medium.com/@annalienk

Marshall, T. (1992). *The meaning of liberty: Thurgood Marshall's stirring acceptance speech after receiving the prestigious Liberty Award on July 4, 1992*. NAACP Legal Fund. https://www.naacpldf.org/press-release/thurgood-marshalls-stirring-acceptance-speech-after-receiving-the-prestigious-liberty-award-on-july-4-1992/

Mitchell, M. (2016). Finding the "prism": Understanding Vygotsky's "perezhivanie" as an ontogenetic unit of child consciousness. *International Research in Early Childhood Education, 7*(1), 5–33.

Oluo, I. (n.d.). Center for children & youth justice. https://ccyj.org/wp-content/uploads/2020/06z/2020-06-08-CCYJ-Black-Lives-Matter-Statement.pdf

Palmer, P. J. (2007). *The courage to teach: Exploring the inner landscape of a teacher's life*. Jossey-Bass.

Schön, D. (1983). *The reflective practitioner: How professionals think in action*. Basic Books.

Schön, D. (1987). *Educating the reflective practitioner: Toward a new design for teaching and learning in the professions*. Jossey-Bass.

Shah, N., & Coles, J. (2020). Preparing teachers to notice race in classrooms: Contextualizing the competencies of preservice teachers with antiracist inclinations. *Journal of Teacher Education, 71*(5), 584–599. https://doi.org/10.1177/0022487119900204

Solorzano, D. G., & Bernal, D. D. (2001). Examining transformational resistance through critical and LatCrit theory framework: Chicana and Chicano students in an urban context. *Urban Education, 36*(3), 308–342. https://doi.org/10.1177/0042085901363002

United States of America, Pledge of Allegiance. (1892). https://usa.usembassy.de/government-pledge.htm

Valencia, R. (2010). *Dismantling contemporary deficit thinking: Educational thought and practice*. Taylor & Francis.

Vygotsky, L. (1935/1994). The problem of the environment. In R. van der Veer & J. Valsiner (Eds.), *The Vygotsky reader* (pp. 338–354). Blackwell. (Original work published 1935)

Wallace-Wells, B. (June 10, 2021). What do conservatives fear about Critical Race Theory? *The New Yorker*. https://www.newyorker.com/news/annals-of-inquiry/what-do-conservatives-fear-about-critical-race-theory

Watts, R., Griffith, D., & Abdul-Adil, J. (1999). Sociopolitical development as an antidote for oppression: Theory and action. *American Journal of Community Psychology, 27*(2), 255–272. https://doi.org/10.1023/A:1022839818873

Webster, A. (2021). *Are you moving through the world inclusively or exclusively?* [Key note address], Association of Teacher Educators (ATE) Summer Conference (online).

Wilkerson, I. (2020). *Caste: The origins of our discontents*. Random House.

Chapter 2

Situating the Self in Context

Co-teaching to Prepare Antiracist Teachers to Teach in Urban Settings

Laura Renzi and Matthew Kruger-Ross

In this chapter, two White co-teacher educators showcase two antiracist teaching practices that were used in a 12 credit, 2-course summer residency program created to prepare science, technology, engineering, and mathematics (STEM) teachers for urban contexts. Our work is influenced by two bodies of theoretical scholarship: the trajectory of antiracist scholarship and the use of critical friendships in self-study and action research. Here we discuss two practices used in our MEd summer course. These practices can be framed as a process of simultaneously (a) introducing students to the larger and complex narrative surrounding antiracism while also (b) encouraging them to purposefully reflect on their own identities. We continue to ask ourselves how we can help these future teachers connect all of these pieces to antiracist pedagogies in the classroom.

INTRODUCTION

George Floyd was murdered by the police on Monday, May 25, 2020. At 9:00 a.m. on May 26, 2020, our work as co-teaching teacher educators and critical friends began. While preparing a new master's program for future urban teachers, we had been focused on building culturally relevant practices and pedagogies into the coursework from the ground up. But with the dramatic shift in the national consciousness in connection with race and police violence, all activities, readings, and minilessons had to be rethought in order to meet the historical moment: We needed antiracist pedagogy.

In this chapter, we, two White co-teacher educators, showcase two antiracist teaching practices that were used in a 12 credit, 2-course summer residency program created to prepare STEM teachers for urban contexts. What brought us together to begin this co-teaching journey was a redesign of an MEd program with initial teaching certification that was to prepare future teachers to teach in urban contexts. Complicating the matter was the program being moved to a virtual space due to COVID-19 in spring 2020.

While we come from different academic and subject area backgrounds, not to mention departments (which are notoriously siloed within academia), we have cultivated a space within the intersection of our research and teaching interests to complete truly critical work with future teachers. Having worked within social-justice-oriented teaching for most of our careers, the work in this new MEd program was a natural extension of our mutual commitment to social justice teaching in the K–12 classroom. What formed from this collaboration was not just a personal friendship and co-teaching relationship, but the start of a critical friendship through the reading of Ibram X. Kendi's *How to be an antiracist*. Our teaching focused on Kendi's work detailing the structural history of racism within the United States (2017), but also his more recent scholarship on developing and sustaining an antiracist way of being in the world (2019).

Our teaching practice is influenced by two bodies of theoretical scholarship: the trajectory of antiracist scholarship and the use of critical friendships in self-study and action research. Continued readings and critical conversations in antiracism practice have led us to reimagine our approach to teacher education methods and pedagogy.

THEORETICAL BACKGROUND

Scholarship and teacher research in the area of what is now called antiracism has a robust history that spans at least four (if not more) decades. To be sure, this history is rich and multifaceted, complex and intricate, and we will not be able to do justice to it in this brief chapter. To begin, Gloria Ladson-Billings's (1995, 1998) foundational work on critical race theory and education, as well as Peggy McIntosh's (1989) conceptualizing of White privilege, marks an important early scholarship into the question of how educators should work to address issues of power, privilege, and race. We would be remiss to not acknowledge that there have been many names associated with this scholarly narrative, including multicultural education and diversity, to culturally relevant pedagogy and critical race theory. At present the narrative has shifted to include antiracism (Kendi, 2019) and antiracist pedagogies (Blakeney, 2005; Wagner, 2005). Most recently there have been calls to use the language of abolitionist teaching to name this area of practice and scholarship (Love, 2019). The shifting vocabulary are attempts to name a thread of scholarship that seeks to explore the intersectionality of race, education, teachers, and curriculum and are waypoints along a journey of ever-increasing clarity and understanding in describing both the history of systems of oppression and their impact on education. From this stance, antiracism seems to be the best language at present to describe this work while recognizing that these ideas are connected to a larger historical context.

A number of fundamental approaches and distinctions identified by other scholars of race and education provide the context for the theoretical framework of this chapter. These include unpacking and critiquing Whiteness (Bush, 2011), addressing White fragility (DiAngelo, 2018, 2021), accounting for and addressing emotions connected to race and education (Matias, 2016), abolitionist teaching (Love, 2020), and the intersection of niceness and Whiteness (Castagno, 2014). The significance of Kendi's (2019) contribution to antiracist understanding is crucial as well. Antiracism is not a fixed state but a continual process of interrogation, a journey that begins with the personal but also recognizes and challenges systemic and systematic racism and oppression (DiAngelo, 2021). The present self-study takes up the project of antiracist work within teacher education to explore how to prepare future teachers not only to be antiracist, but also to be teacher-researchers who are equipped to critically reflect on their practice using self-study methods (Pinnegar & Hamilton, 2009).

Of particular interest for our work as antiracist teacher educators is that we are practicing antiracist pedagogies in front of our students, "breaking the fourth wall," to borrow a metaphor from film studies. One of the common threads from Whiteness studies includes the necessary personal interrogations that White-identified individuals must do to contribute equitably to the whole of antiracism (Castagno, 2014; DiAngelo, 2021; Matias, 2016). In short, White people cannot rely on Black and Brown colleagues to *teach* or *explain* their experiences of oppression and disempowerment. These narratives are, of course, helpful and insightful, but White people must acknowledge that it is our responsibility to name, critique, analyze, and deconstruct our White identities and explore (and challenge) the ways that our identities contribute and sustain systems of White supremacy and privilege. By demonstrating for our students (i.e., by "breaking the fourth wall") our own work as teacher educators and our continuing and unfinished journeys to become antiracist pedagogues, we showcase the work of not only antiracism but also critically reflective practice. One frame we use to inform this is critical friends.

Unique to our approach is that we simultaneously serve as both co-teachers and as critical friends for one another in our work together in antiracist pedagogies. Co-teaching exists on a spectrum from two (or more) teachers teaching the same subject or course independently and in separate locations, modalities, and times, to true co-teaching where two (or more) instructors teach the same students in the same location and at the same time. In our current co-teaching relationship we practice on the latter end of the spectrum, coming from similar educational backgrounds and sharing assumptions about teaching and learning. The subject matter, teacher education methods, and antiracist pedagogies, we would argue, might actually be best taught in a co-teaching arrangement. What is more, by purposefully cultivating critical friendship between co-teachers, we argue that the co-teaching relationship is strengthened in such a way that teaching and learning of students is impacted positively.

In addition to co-teaching, we also serve as critical friends. Serving as a critical friend is a keystone to self-study research (Samaras, 2011) and action research (Stieha, 2014), and we borrow liberally from these traditions of teacher education research to inform our understanding of this relationship. To be a critical friend is not simply adhering to the everyday idea of a best friend or long-term trusted colleague, although these also overlap. A critical friend is a person who can serve as a critical listening and dialogue partner for a teacher or instructor (Costa & Kallick, 1993). A critical friend relationship begins with an invitation, builds with open and honest communication, and requires trust building, boundary setting, and explicit expectations (Stieha, 2014).

While we draw simultaneously from self-study and action research traditions, with regard to our enacting of critical friendship we have explored primarily self-study methodologies for our research. Drawing on Samaras (2011), we are reminded that self-study teacher research is (a) personal situated inquiry, (b) critical collaborative inquiry, (c) improved learning, (d) a transparent and systematic research process, and (e) knowledge generation and presentation. For example, we work together as critical friends ((b), critical collaborative inquiry) to plan activities that invite our students to join us in a self-study methodological approach. Our aim is to share our self-study work openly with our students ((e), knowledge generation and presentation) to help them engage with themselves and their work as teacher-researchers. By building on structured journaling, class discussion, interviews, and other scripted activities ((d), systematic research process), we hope to have our students continue the antiracist framework modeled in our teaching practices throughout the yearlong program and into their own future classrooms. In the following section, we present and describe a two-pronged approach to antiracist teacher education practice that we have found successful in our work together as co-teachers and critical friends.

ANTIRACIST TEACHER EDUCATION PRACTICES AND IMPLEMENTATION

In this section we describe two antiracist practices that have emerged from our classrooms. They might seem obvious, but it was only upon further reflection on our pedagogical practice that we uncovered the specific strategies we were implementing with our preservice teacher candidates. Put briefly, the two practices can be framed as a process of simultaneously (a) introducing students to the larger and complex narrative and scholarly conversation surrounding antiracism while also (b) encouraging our future teachers to purposefully reflect on their own identities. This section introduces and unpacks both of these practices that we name "situating the self in context," as they have been implemented in our co-taught teacher education methods course with graduate-level, STEM preservice teachers.

A brief note on our lived context is helpful before we describe these ideas further. Our primary teaching in antiracism emerges from our co-teaching of an interdisciplinary MEd program that began in May 2020. We had planned for two years with our colleagues to implement the new program face-to-face. However, in March 2020 our university announced that right after spring break all courses would transition to fully remote for the remainder of the spring term due to COVID-19. It seems strange to reflect back on this moment, but at the beginning of April 2020 we actually thought we might be able to have face-to-face courses in late May when the new master's program began. This was not to be, of course, as the administration announced remote instruction in late April for all summer courses as well. Thus, in the span of less than three weeks we had to transition: The whole program now had to be conducted online. It seems quaint to reflect back now, but at the time we had little to no understanding of COVID-19 and its impact on U.S. society that we now know in late 2021.

As of this writing we have taught two cohorts of students in the master's program completely online. In the first cohort, we taught 14 students with a majority of students in STEM subject areas. The second cohort has 23 students with 19 STEM students and 4 humanities students. The cohorts included students with varying backgrounds (e.g., racial, ethnic, socioeconomic, geographic, gender identity) and dispositions toward teaching, but both participated in approximately the same course assignments and readings. With a few exceptions, the preservice teachers were White, young (just graduated undergraduate programs), and suburban based.

The first antiracism practice in our program is introducing preservice teachers to the context of antiracism. By context we mean not only thematizing and reflecting on the current climate and headlines they are seeing in the news, but also the historical, cultural, and scholarly narrative that grounds and provides a boundary for antiracist pedagogies. As these are graduate students, we have chosen substantial texts to serve in this role. For our teaching thus far, Kendi's *How to be an antiracist* has served as the foundational text.

Kendi's approach, we think, is what truly helped frame our teaching, personally and professionally, and provided a framework for discussions with our future teachers. He begins by laying out fundamental definitions that help to distinguish antiracism that he uses to connect throughout the remainder of the book. In fact, each chapter opens with a set of definitions of terms that becomes the focus of the chapter. Arguably, the key definitions are about racism and antiracism; for example, "Racist: One who is supporting a racist policy through their actions or inaction or expressing a racist idea. / Antiracist: One who is supporting an antiracist policy through their actions or expressing an antiracist idea" (2019, p. 9). By opening the book with such a clear and distinct framework, Kendi helps to ground what will become difficult and complex conversations in definitional terms. The question always returns to "Is this racist or antiracist?" Kendi's book then traces a path through other related terms and ideas, such as double consciousness and assimilationist/segregationist, before connecting gender and other anti-oppressive practices to antiracist work.

As an alternative text, we have also used *Stamped* as a foundational text for situating preservice teachers within the context of antiracism. There are actually two versions of *Stamped*: one originally written by Kendi and a second written by Jason Reynolds (along with Kendi) (2020) that is framed for adolescents. Whereas *How to be an antiracist* focuses primarily on the present day, *Stamped* takes the longer, historical view while tracing the history of racist ideas and policies throughout U.S. and world history. Both texts meet our criteria of serving as a foundational experience for preservice teachers to uncover and immerse themselves in the context of antiracist work and scholarship.

The second antiracist teacher education practice that we have implemented is what we term identity work. We require our preservice teachers to carefully and thoughtfully begin mapping their social, racial, and ethnic identities using a reflective journal to chronicle this journey. This reflective journal is kept as a shared Google Folder that is viewable only by both of us and the student. This provides privacy but also allows us to have a continual dialogue with the student.

Specifically, before we read Kendi, students are asked to complete activities from Tiffany Jewell's *This book is antiracist* in their reflective journal that provides an opportunity for them to interrogate their social identities as well as to identify their racial and ethnic identities. These activities challenge students to look at the areas within their identities where they experience privilege (or oppression) because of those identities. Students also use their identities to create a visual representation through the use of Keynote slides and clipart. This activity situates students so that they can see themselves and their place within the conversations around race and antiracism. It also allows us to see where the class ranges regarding self-identification, but also in knowledge and reflection about their place in society.

One of the key takeaways from Kendi's text (2019) is that antiracist work and pedagogy is not a level or identity you achieve, whereby once you have unlocked a certain understanding you have completed the work that must be done. You do not, by reading *this* number of books on antiracist practice and watching *this* number of hours of documentaries, magically become antiracist. Antiracism is a way of life, a way of teaching that is a continual process; it is a process of reflective practice, and it must be purposeful (DiAngelo, 2021; Kendi, 2019).

When we assign the Kendi text, we include two additional scaffolds for students: benchmarked dates and required journaling prompts. *How to be an antiracist* is not a reading that can be completed in one sitting, not only because of its length, but because a true reading of the text requires work on the self. For example, this work includes self-reflection on one's identities, context, and personal histories. We typically assign the book in 3–4 sections with roughly 4–5 chapters in each section across three weeks. Every other day we have preservice teachers complete journal reflections using guiding questions we have selected from Kendi's (2020) supplementary publication devoted to personal journaling. Students are required to chronicle their reading in their reflective journals. Here are a few of the journal prompts:

- Have you ever described yourself as "not racist"? What does "not racist" mean to you? Why do you think so many people are invested in believing that they are "not racist"?
- How does our focus on the White people as the problem instead of racist power and policy lead to the strengthening of racist power and policy?
- Why is facing facts and accepting new knowledge essential to being antiracist?

In reading and working through Kendi (as well as other social justice/ antiracist theorist's work), it is not enough to read about someone else's experiences. Interrogating the self is a key step in understanding one's place in society, and by understanding one's place in society we can move toward understanding how society functions on a larger scale. With that in mind, we strategically and methodically plan identity activities that ask our candidates to reflect on their own upbringing with regard to race, class, gender expression, and so forth and how those identities affect their education, choices, and memories of schooling.

One activity students complete is a "Where I Am From" poem using the identities expressed in the reflective journal. To begin, Laura models the process of composing the poem, using their own poem as an example. Then, students identify elements of Laura's identities using the poem as evidence. As they begin to draft their own "Where I Am From" poems, students are not given any restrictions with regard to number of lines or stanzas, but rather are able to represent their culture, childhood, family structure, and so forth, in whatever way they choose. See a sample below from a student.

Sample "Where I Am From" Poem
I am from wanderlust
New cities and new houses
Exciting adventures and family trips

I am from afternoon tea
Scones and clotted cream after school
Chats with my mother about her home across the sea

I am from suburbia
Split level houses and cul de sacs
Driving busy roads past constant construction

I am from neverending learning
Postgrad parents and gifts of books
Visiting cathedrals and castles whenever possible

I am from concert goers
Mp3s, records, and CDs
Blasting all genres through the house

I am from hooligans
Screaming and crying in front of the TV
Watching England lose on penalties

When Laura shares her poem, she guides students through a series of discussion prompts that begins with: What can you tell about me from reading my poem? Preservice teachers are able to identify her socioeconomic status, gender, and ethnic identity. Laura pushes students further by asking them to consider where her race is present in the poem and how they were able to identify this identity. Often, this includes an indication of the various privileges that are embedded in the text of Laura's poem, such as having a two-parent household with a scientist father and housewife mother. The two antiracist practices truly work in tandem as students are guided between experiences of self-reflection (as in the "Where I Am From" poem) and the larger, theoretical texts that situate the systemic work in antiracism.

An example of using film as text includes having students watch the 2004 movie *Crash*. When we introduce the viewing assignment to students, we begin by exploring the metaphorical meaning around the movie's title. The plot can be seen as a series of various people who literally *crash* into each other in Los Angeles in their daily lives in the early 2000s. The cast is multiracial, multiethnic, and multilingual. There are literal car accidents, as well as representations of criminals, police officers, upscale socialites, and a district attorney. The movie highlights the ways these various characters' lives intersect. One takeaway is how judgment, racism, classism, and sexism fuel not only relationships, but those reactions and interactions we have with people throughout life. Although we recognize the limitations of this movie, and acknowledge that the movie has its critics, we also advocate for it as a starting point to crucial conversations with our students about race, stereotyping, and as an entry point into insights from Kendi's *How to be an antiracist*.

As students weave their identities and situate themselves into the larger societal context, their self-reflection of becoming a teacher becomes more real when they are asked to draft their first positionality statement. In their response journal they are asked to write a brief summative statement of who they are in terms of their identities and how these identities will inform their practice as a teaching professional. We encourage them, even if it is only initial thoughts, to start to acknowledge that, for example, being a male makes a difference in your being a teacher, being White makes a difference in being a teacher. The positionality is further informed by a belief statement activity. Students are asked to rank 10 aspects of teaching from 1 to 10—1 being most important, 10 being least important. These aspects of teaching include classroom culture, content/subject area, equity and equality, technology, discussion and conversation, school and community relationships, teacher self-reflection, parents, students, and evaluation of student learning. While we know that there are many other aspects of teaching, this somewhat arbitrary list helps to focus their attention. From this ranking, students create belief statements by using a sentence starter: I believe that [students/technology/classroom culture] have a . . . because [. . .]. For example, "I believe my classroom and the community have a mutual obligation for support and growth because . . . ." These belief statements elucidate their ideas of how different aspects of teaching will play a role in their future classroom. These identity pieces, including the "Where I Am From" poem, the positionality statement, and the belief statements, become the foundation for the first draft of their teaching philosophy.

One of the last pieces in this identity work is for students to create a professional development plan to chronicle their journey of continued learning and development in areas where they have interest or need/want to gain more knowledge. This professional development plan consists of membership in their professional organization, the reading of one book or series of articles, engaging with a podcast or movie, participating in a professional development opportunity in the form of a workshop or webinar, and reflections on all of these items. In the professional development plan, it is the student's responsibility to make the connections between their own identity and what they need to continue to explore within the larger narrative of antiracist pedagogies and practices. For example, they are required to read a book or series of articles and multimedia, but the texts must be focused on an antiracist practice. The professional development opportunity is chosen by them to expand their own practice as a future teacher and could be an exploration of alternative assessment or a new technology tool. The goal of this assignment is to set up the future teachers for success as we acknowledge the importance of ongoing professional development in the career of a teacher. We also encourage students to view the professional development plan as their professional responsibility to continue the work we have only just started, situating the self in context.

REFLECTION ON EFFECTIVENESS OF PRACTICE

As co-teachers and critical friends we are continuously reflecting and critiquing our pedagogical choices and the execution of our activities daily. We are in a constant state of reflection. This can even occur in informal settings and manners, including late night emails or messages to reflect on a learning activity that did not go quite to plan, or an idea for a future reading that might work better the next time a lesson is taught. In this section, we focus on a few takeaways from our teaching. There are many other examples we could have chosen, but we have selected these because we think they exemplify common concerns of other teacher educators.

First, we return over and over again to reflect on the difficulty we have estimating the amount of time, energy, reflection, and capacity it takes to prepare future teachers. We would note that teaching introductory methods (lesson planning, objectives, activities, assessing learning) is challenging and all consuming, and this is already in addition to any antiracist pedagogies. For example, within our lived context, we are working with future teachers on their teacher identities, how these identities play into the larger society, and how this influences their classroom. But, we are also responsible for general methods, such as lesson planning, and threading the connections in the classroom to educational psychology and adolescent development, special education, and educational technology. To complicate matters further, this is a 12-month program; however, we are only involved in the first two months. The coursework includes the first courses in the students' program.

The stated goal of the course is to introduce general teacher methods for working in urban settings. We also simultaneously integrate the two antiracist practices. Ultimately, and in best practice, over the course of 10 weeks we attempt to weave general methods, antiracist practices, and the identity work we know to be important for future teachers to be successful both in general methods, and as future antiracist pedagogues. The most challenging aspect of this work is that antiracist pedagogies and practices are not like a traditional content area that can be taught and prescribed in a specified time frame because (a) it is ongoing and (b) it is tied intimately to the identity of the students. In order to teach someone to work in an urban setting and to utilize antiracist practices, teacher educators must have students interrogate their own internal biases and prejudices, as well as examine the lenses in which they see society and ultimately their students and education as a whole. We continue to struggle with how to balance time, how to integrate these pieces together, which activity gets more attention, and so forth.

Second, there is a disconnect between the identity work and learning activities that we have our future teachers complete, and how they continue to work to understand what teaching is both existentially and literally. By this we mean what teaching is as a profession, and what a teacher does in their classroom on a daily basis with students. In the first few weeks of the course, we have students complete reflective journal entries and participate in activities (alone and together) that help them unpack, describe, and critique their assumptions about the profession of teaching and what it is teachers do. For example, we have them journal about their favorite teacher from high school and reflect on what they liked about the teacher, their pedagogical practices, and their disposition in the classroom. We also have students explore a number of metaphors about teaching (e.g., teacher as gardener, teacher as coach, etc.) to help them better start to grasp and provide language for the daily practices teachers engage in.

However, when students begin in the second half of the course to lesson plan and plot out their curriculum in a unit plan, we have realized that they are unable to make the crucial connections between the foundational contextual work in antiracism and identity, and the pedagogical strategies used in their lesson plans. For instance, when we review their lesson plan drafts, students lean heavily on the language of the content standards and utilize traditional teaching methods such as lecturing and assessment strategies like assigning quizzes/tests rather than developing and implementing an antiracist-informed pedagogical stance in the classroom. This demonstrates that our earlier identity work is still ongoing and that these connections have not yet fully been established. We continue to ask ourselves how we can help these future teachers connect all of these pieces to antiracist pedagogies in the classroom. Since we cannot do the work of antiracism without supporting them in doing their own identity work, it is almost as if the course runs out of time (while we run out of steam and patience) to guide and facilitate them along this journey.

In reflection, we understand that building a teacher identity is a journey and not something that can realistically be secured in a 10-week course. We know that when it comes to unpacking identity, antiracism, and social justice concerns, everyone starts at a different point. Thus, we also realize that everyone is going to end at a different point. Everyone's growth and reflection is of their own making, and so it takes some people longer to do that work. Because they are not yet teachers and have not been in the classroom of their own, it is also hard for us to activate prior knowledge of teaching without them returning to memories of their own educational experiences, both in K–12 and college. For example, many of our future teachers, because of their previous work in their content areas, both K–12 and college, resist and continually ask how to implement antiracist pedagogies in STEM courses. They claim they have never seen these practices before and therefore assume it is not possible. What is more, many are not automatically inclined to ambiguity, discussion-based course work, and student-centered learning—as students and future teachers. In order for us to know what we are doing is actually making a difference in our future teachers, we need to follow them into the classroom to see if, how, and in what ways these pedagogies are integrated into their teaching.

MOVING FORWARD

As we pivot from our second cohort, we have recently been reflecting on how we almost feel like first-year teachers again. We have been, for many weeks, treading water, staying late in Zoom sessions to revise lesson plans for the next day, and unpacking class sessions and discussions. Rather than thriving, we have largely been in survival mode. We have been considering whether or not this is because of the emotional intensity of antiracist pedagogies, or if teaching cohorts of students in Zoom for 16+ months has truly taken its toll. Research readily recognizes the emotional labor that must be honored and unpacked whenever naming and challenging White supremacy and systemic oppression (Matias, 2016). And, as referenced earlier, we have been teaching preservice teachers utilizing antiracist pedagogies online and in small Zoom boxes rather than in person and in the community.

Nonetheless, these were challenges that inspired us to take our co-teaching relationship to the next level as critical friends. Together, we have been able to critically reflect and uncover a few hard truths related to our practice. For example, we know that preservice teachers cannot learn to do antiracist pedagogies in 10 weeks, in one course, without a context, and without students. At this point we also know that exploring these ideas in a course remains theoretical for them. We know antiracist work is not as simple as reading a book or completing an activity. It is also realizing that these preservice teachers are unsure of how to lesson plan, cannot distinguish between an outcome and an objective, and find it hard to visualize a curriculum—much less integrate antiracist pedagogies. We continue to have future preservice teachers push back on our calls for integrating antiracist work, claiming that antiracism might be a better fit in humanities courses. Therefore, we have realized that we need to interrogate all the various components of the coursework (e.g., identity work, antiracist pedagogy, lesson planning, curriculum, classroom culture, student development) in the classroom context.

As a result, we are following several students through their program and into their field experiences. We want to continue to be present for them to push and question. We want to coach them in using antiracist pedagogies in their classroom using reflective practices. One such reflective practice we have already setup with them is having them select and cultivate a critical friendship with one of their peers. Exploring this next step in our work requires a more structured research practice to conduct interviews and observations of these future teachers. Reflecting back on Kendi's work we know that antiracism is not a point to reach, but rather an ongoing journey that must be continually renewed. We remain committed to pushing each other, as colleagues and critical friends, to interrogate our practice as antiracist teachers and reflect on how we can model and facilitate conversations with our students to prepare them to become antiracist teachers as well.

REFERENCES

Blakeney, A. M. (2005). Antiracist pedagogy: Definition, theory, and professional development. *Journal of Curriculum and Pedagogy, 2*(1), 119–132. https://doi.org/10.1080/15505170.2005.10411532

Bush, M. E. L. (2011). *Everyday forms of whiteness: Understanding race in a 'post-racial' world.* Rowman & Littlefield.

Castagno, A. E. (2014). *Educated in whiteness: Good intentions and diversity in schools.* University of Minnesota Press.

Costa, A. L., & Kallick, B. (1993). Through the lens of a critical friend. *Educational Leadership, 51*(2), 49–51.

DiAngelo, R. (2018). *White fragility: Why it's so hard for white people to talk about racism.* Beacon Press.

DiAngelo, R. (2021). *Nice racism: How progressive white people perpetuate racial harm.* Beacon Press.

Kendi, I. X. (2017). *Stamped from the beginning: The definitive history of racist ideas in America.* Bold Type Books.

Kendi, I. X. (2019). *How to be an antiracist.* One World.

Kendi, I. X. (2020). *Be antiracist: A journal for awareness, reflection, and action.* One World.

Ladson-Billings, G. (1995). Toward a theory of culturally relevant pedagogy. *American Educational Research Journal, 32*(3), 465–491. https://doi.org/10.3102/00028312032003465

Ladson-Billings, G. (1998). Just what is critical race theory and what's it doing in a nice field like education? *International Journal of Qualitative Studies in Education, 11*(1), 7–24. https://doi.org/10.1080/095183998236863

Love, B. (2019, May 23). How schools are 'spirit murdering' black and brown students. *Education Week.* https://www.edweek.org/leadership/opinion-how-schools-are-spirit-murdering-black-and-brown-students/2019/05

Love, B. (2020). *We want to do more than survive: Abolitionist teaching and the pursuit of educational freedom.* Beacon Press.

Matias, C. E. (2016). *Feeling white: Whiteness, emotionality, and education.* Sense/Brill.

McIntosh, P. (1989). White privilege: Unpacking the invisible knapsack. *Peace and Freedom Magazine,* 10–12. https://nationalseedproject.org/Key-SEED-Texts/white-privilege-unpacking-the-invisible-knapsack

Pinnegar, S., & Hamilton, M. L. (2009). *Self-study practice as a genre of qualitative research.* Springer.

Reynolds, J., & Kendi, I. X. (2020). *Stamped: Racism, antiracism and you.* Little Brown Books for Young Readers.

Samaras, A. (2011). *Self-study teacher research.* SAGE Publications.

Stieha, V. (2014). Critical friend. In D. Coghlan & M. Brydon-Miller (Eds.), *The SAGE Encyclopedia of Action Research* (pp. 207–208). SAGE Publications.

Wagner, A. E. (2005). Unsettling the academy: Working through the challenges of anti-racist pedagogy. *Race Ethnicity and Education, 8*(3), 261–275. https://doi.org/10.1080/13613320500174333

Chapter 3

L.I.S.T.E.N. Up

Antibias/Antiracist Orientations in Teacher Education

Danné E. Davis and Sumi Hagiwara

Because racism from society seeps into higher education, it is essential for all faculty, particularly those preparing future teachers, to adopt two practices. One is to challenge anti-Black and anti-Asian American Pacific Islanders (AAPIs) racist sentiments in their work. The other practice is to position future teachers to embrace appropriate antiracist strategies for classroom use. L.I.S.T.E.N. is offered as a tool to reimagine antibias and antiracist (ABAR) work. Drawing on Milner's (2007) analyses of the intersection of race, culture, and researcher positionality toward racial and cultural consciousness, there are six orientations of associative heuristic tools: Learn Correct Names and Pronouns, Implement Inclusive Leadership, Show Love (and Understanding), Tell Your Story, Exclude Euphemisms, and Navigate New Spaces. L.I.S.T.E.N. is designed to advance teacher education faculty and leaders toward inclusive practice and away from bias and racist actions.

INTRODUCTION

We are women teacher-scholars—one Black[1] American; one Japanese American—both tenured at the same predominantly White institution (PWI) in the northeast. Like most educators, the Summer of Racial Reckoning[2] combined with a global pandemic made for an unprecedented fall 2020 semester launch. The numerous deaths of Black and AAPIs and social unrest compelled us to reimagine ABAR work by and for our colleagues, students, and academicians at PWIs, including our institution. Upon reflection of our racial lives in our workplace, this discussion is offered as a resource, especially for instructors and leaders in teacher education to move beyond gap-gazing to implement six ABAR orientations of praxis. This chapter contributes to extant literature on diversity and answers the call for antiracist work.

ANTIRACISM AGENDA IN TEACHER EDUCATION

Because racism from society seeps into higher education, it is essential for all faculty, particularly those preparing future teachers, to adopt two practices. One is to challenge anti-Black and anti-AAPI racist applications in their teaching and second, to position future teachers to practice appropriate antiracist strategies for use with future school children. The practices are especially necessary given recent spikes in U.S. hate crimes motivated by race. According to FBI Hate Crime Statistics, anti-Black violence incidents rose 6% or 7,759 cases reported in 2020 (Hernandez, 2021). Since March 2020, the national coalition Stop AAPI Hate notes 4,548 reports of racial attacks targeting AAPI people in the United States (Yellow Horse et al., 2021). Additional data from the Center for the Study of Hate and Extremism show a 150% increase in hate crimes directed at members of the AAPI community (Yang, 2021). As in the past, the fear today is that People of Color and their allies will act to destabilize the dominant White culture—for example, White supremacy. We seek to decenter the fragility of Whiteness and center our work specifically against anti-Black and anti-Asian racism, countering biases, tackling prejudices, and dismantling ideologies of superiority over people of African and Asian ancestries (Alexander, 2021).

Antiracist work counters "any measures that produce or sustain racial inequity between racial groups" (Kendi, 2020, p. 18). Kendi explains *measures* as "written and unwritten laws, rules, procedures, processes, regulations, and guidelines" (p. 18) devised to unfairly impact one group based on their race. The teacher certification system is an example of a racist measure against Black candidates. To teach in any public school in the United States, educators are required to have a state-issued license and a minimum of a bachelor's degree from an accredited institution of higher education. However, this college degree requirement is especially biased against Black candidates. Black students experience lower high school and college graduation rates, making a career in teaching nearly impossible to attain (Figlio, 2018; Villegas & Davis, 2007). According to the National Center for Education Statistics (2021) during 2018–2019, 80% of Black students graduate high school compared to 89% White and 93% Asian Pacific Islanders. During the same period, the college enrollment rate was 59% Asian, 42% White, and 37% Black.

In addition to access to college, another barrier to accessing a career in teaching is earning passing Praxis rates, the state licensure test required for certification. The Black candidate pass rate was 52%, whereas White candidates passed approximately 87% (Gitomer et al., 2011). The data calls into question how the educational system is setting up Black students to pursue a career in teaching.

Historically, licensure ensures that school children receive quality education and minimizes unfair job competition (LaBue, 1960). Today's reality indicates both outcomes as unfulfilled. Instead, reports show teachers with earned college degrees using developmentally inappropriate methods and delivering racially offensive content. Licensed teachers are also documented leading Middle Passage simulations and slave auction block reenactments (Herron, 2019) with Black students playing the role of the enslaved. Racist rhetoric directed at AAPI K–12 students also goes unaddressed (Truong et al., 2021). These failed claims of living history activities by teachers do not exemplify spaces of quality education.

Teacher hiring practices are also questionable. Today Black and AAPI K–12 teachers are underrepresented in the teaching profession (Brennan, 2016; Figlio, 2018). Citing data from the National Center of Education Statistics, the percentages of public school teachers in 2017–2018 were 7% Black and 2% AAPIs (Schaeffer, 2021). D'amico et al. (2017) found a district's hiring practices that showed a pattern of Black applicants less likely to be offered a position compared to their White counterparts. When Black teachers are hired, they are more likely to be placed in schools characterized as struggling, with large populations of children of color and learners living in poverty (Milner, 2007). Conversely, the "model minority myth" (Yi & Todd, 2021) that suggests AAPIs inherently have high "intellectual quotients" and natural proclivity for "science, technology, engineering, and mathematics" misinterprets AAPI educators as apathetic, uncompassionate, and ill equipped to manage sociocultural matters among schoolchildren (Bergey, 2021). The model minority "stereotype . . . affects the work of Asian American teachers, their identities, and their pedagogy . . . to a post-model minority moment" (Chow, 2017, p. 2); the discriminatory trope "intensifies racism toward [AAPIs]" (Kim, 2007, p. 568). Upon hiring teachers, school personnel need to develop accurate understandings of the cultural affinity nuances as well as the lived experiences of Black and AAPI educators joining the school community. Regardless of racial identity, all learners benefit from having teachers of color (D'amico et al., 2017). Teachers with African and Japanese heritage are uniquely positioned to draw on their lived experience to meet learning outcomes especially as they pertain to African and Japanese culture but not solely.

Although we acknowledge our tenured status totaling a combined 36 years in higher education, Black and AAPI scholars are sorely underrepresented in the academy. Among full-time faculty, Blacks represent 5.7% and AAPIs,

9.5% (Johnson, 2017). In the role of department chair, during the 2018–2019 academic year, AAPIs represented 6.5% and Blacks 4% (ACE, 2017). At the level of college and university president, AAPIs accounted for 2.3% with 7.9% represented by Blacks (ACE, 2017). The lack of opportunity for Black and AAPI faculty to enhance their capacity and social capital to compete for mobility within the existing system successfully reifies the existence of PWIs and the uneven distribution of power, wealth, and opportunity across race (Stein & Andreotti, 2016). We call into question the disparity between faculty and administrator demographics compared to that of their students. Despite attempts to eliminate biased thinking and behavior to recruit diverse candidates (Griffin et al., 2020; O'Meara et al., 2020), Asian and Black academics have a minimal presence in the higher education community. In the context of PWI of higher education, power and privilege are embedded in the executive establishment that perpetuates a dominant culture that normalizes microaggressions and macroaggressions against People of Color.

Black bodies do not feel settled around "[W]hite ones, for reasons that are all too obvious: the long, brutal history of enslavement and subjugation; racial profiling by police; . . . the habitual grind of everyday disregard, discrimination, institutional disrespect . . . and micro-aggressions" (Menakem, 2017, p. 13). Yet, African Americans are not alone as targets of cultural oppression. Despite the benefits gained by AAPIs from occasional "honorary [W]hite" (Yi & Nicholson, 2021) status, since 1790 people of Japanese ancestry have faced nativistic racism—for example, bias in favor of White American patriotism. A wholly "outsider" Japanese in America experience has meant being "barred from becoming naturalized citizens, prohibited from owning or leasing land . . . marrying [W]hites in some states, and harassed, driven out, and segregated from the rest of America" (Lee, 2015, p. 8). The words *alien* and *enemy* still appear as language in official U.S. immigration policies. Moreover, elected 21st century national leaders routinely spew ethnic tropes and racial epithets reminiscent of 19th century anti-Japanese xenophobic hate linked to fear of eventual overthrow of White American social and economic systems (Lee, 2015). People with Japanese ancestry have "been denied equal rights alongside African Americans" (Lee, 2015, p. 8).

"L.I.S.T.E.N. UP": ANTIRACIST TEACHER EDUCATION PRACTICE AND LEADERSHIP

In this section, we discuss our ideological and conceptual beliefs through ABAR orientations dubbed L.I.S.T.E.N., an acronym created as a product of praxis to transform and heal. The six ABAR orientations are not linear but rather are associative heuristic tools designed to advance PWI systems toward healthy, inclusive practice. With these outcomes in mind, educators are urged to:

1. Learn Correct Names and Pronouns
2. Implement Inclusive Leadership
3. Show Love (and Understanding)
4. Tell Your Story
5. Exclude Euphemisms
6. Navigate New Spaces

Learn Correct Names and Pronouns

The 2012 Key and Peele comedy skit, Substitute Teacher, is a must-see to appreciate the value of knowing the names of students and colleagues. The skit depicts Mr. Garvey, an African American teacher, taking attendance of the nearly all-White students in an American history class. Mr. Garvey draws on his familiarity with the pronunciation of Black-sounding names to mispronounce basic names such as Jacqueline and Blake. The skit conveys the significance of people's names. These personal identifiers represent individual identity while reflecting cultural heritage and family pride (Kohli & Solórzano, 2012; Wheeler, 2016). When an educator mispronounces the ethnic name of a student and accurately pronounces the name of White students, the subtle slight may go unnoticed for others, but it lingers for those rendered invisible (Kohli & Solórzano). Moreover, when educators claim that a student's name is difficult to pronounce, or assigns a nickname as an easy alternative, the act veers toward microaggression and linguistic discrimination that can have a lasting impact on a student's well-being and self-identity (Kohli & Solórzano).

Increasingly, institutions are implementing preferred name and inclusive gender pronoun policies. We acknowledge Giroux's caution of "identity politics" (1993, p. 42) simultaneously with noting that "faculty, staff, and university leadership are instrumental in trans students' safety and well-being" (Bauer et al., 2017, p. 4). The University of Vermont is credited as the first institution of higher education to actualize this responsibility in the United States (Howard, 2016), while universities such as ours, Montclair State, a Hispanic Serving Institution in New Jersey, are lauded as a Lesbian, Gay, Bisexual, Trans, and Queer/Questioning-friendly school by Campus Pride Index. Preferred name and inclusive gender pronoun policies help alleviate the emotional weight, personal embarrassment, isolation, and scholastic distraction when transgender voices and identities are forced into the binary and people are compelled into using the language of their oppressors (MacNamara et al., 2017).

Implement Inclusive Leadership

An outcome of recent racial injustices is adopting statements for diversity, equity, and inclusion (DEI). The trend of Indigenous Land acknowledgment and diversity statements on institutional websites and the hiring of DEI leaders to chart a responsive institutional agenda are gaining momentum across disciplines and fields. The challenge with the DEI magic bullet is recognizing that transformation goes beyond statements or creating a position. Enactment of a DEI plan takes place through organizational leaders. As Grace Lee Boggs asserts, "you cannot change any society unless you take responsibility for it unless you see yourself as belonging to it and responsible for changing it" (Harewood & Keefer, 2009, para. 42). Leaders, particularly those who are White, are poised to sit in their racial discomfort to identify ways to build a system and culture that embodies antiracist practice, personally and communally (Menakem, 2017).

An antiracist system and culture reflects a diversity of individuals in the community. By diversifying the faculty, leaders diversify faculty scholarship, inform the development of educational programming, support and mentor a diverse student body, and contribute to course content that reinforces the significance and benefits of a diversified society (Hagedorn et al., 2007; Turner et al., 2008). Faculty support is modeled after trickle-down models where officials in positions of authority, such as provosts, deans, and chairs, influence employees through policies and engagement. "Ultimately, leaders lie at the heart of conveying organizational values and goals" (Marchiondo et al., 2021, p. 2).

To be clear, DEI initiatives, faculty mentoring, and creating opportunities for faculty to cultivate their scholarship are not a means to an end. It is a process by which higher education leaders question *what needs to change*. "Leadership thus embodies the practice of empowering persons to believe that change is necessary and of involving persons with a shared mindset of how to implement change" (Aguirre & Martinez, 2002, p. 55). Higher education leaders have the responsibility to recognize what changes are necessary and to enact policies that institutionalize *how* these changes are sustainable and transformative for an inclusive institutional culture.

Show Love (and Understanding)

Love today is most often associated with romance. It is an intangible object that is nearly impossible to measure. Perhaps for these reasons, love is largely absent from the routines of higher education. In the introduction of *All about Love*, hooks (2018) contends to eradicate racism requires an ethic of love. hooks further suggests that love is an action, something to be done, performed "given its transformative force" (p. 15). The words and work of Rev. Dr. Martin Luther King Jr. offer love to remedy hate and violence. Practicing this type of love coincides with *agapé*, one of several types of love in ancient Greek Philosophy meaning unconditional love. Cochran and Calo (2017) describe this action as selfless, aspirational, deeply empathetic, advancing toward justice and ultimately, right. Agapé is the most humanistic love as it attends to others, without judgment, generalization, and misinformation. Put simply, show empathy to everyone—even to the haters and trolls because it is the right thing to do.

Educators frequently exalt the ethos of Dr. King as an aspirational disposition for meaningful practice. Know that love's transformative power alters the human spirit of other people as it elevates us. It takes a particular temperament to extend favor in the face of adversity—which is part of our personal and professional lived experience.

Alex-Assensoh (2017) asserts that love needs a prominent place in the academy because of its power to do good and inspire goodness. Preparing future teachers to undertake meaningful work in schools with 'Other People's Children' calls for the development of educators' intellectual and emotional capacity to live and work in the community as good neighbors who see color and respect that difference. A sincere message of acceptance or a willingness to practice acceptance contributes to productive classrooms. Leaders in teacher education should show love through genuine words and deeds. Transparent actions benefit the whole.

Tell Your Story

Too often, narratives about individuals are authored by people who may not have an authentic understanding of truth. Chimamanda Ngozi Adichie's (2009) "The Danger of a Single Story" elaborates on the power of authorship emphasizing how "show[ing] a people as one thing, as only one thing, over and over again, and that is what they become" (Adichie, 2009, 9:17). Adichie's words are akin to the outcome of the self-fulfilling prophecy—where repeated false messaging about being and behavior eventually become realized (Salganik & Watts, 2008).

It is not uncommon for a single story to inform how faculty and staff of color are perceived in PWI institutions, informing personnel actions, promotions, and tenure. Likewise, students in a PWI bring single stories of their Black and Asian faculty, who are too often "evaluated more poorly than their [W]hite peers, with Black men faring worse. Faculty members with accents and Asian last names are also penalized. Latinx women are judged more harshly than [W]hite women" (Flagherty, 2021, para. 14). Many variables such as the backlash against low grades, interpersonal conflicts, and racism may attribute to the low reliability of evaluations. The patterns of low scores against faculty of color raise inherent questions of the validity and reliability of student evaluations.

To leverage biases against faculty and staff of color, we assert the significance of talk, telling our stories to inform how others understand our character beyond accents, last names, and skin color. We claim authorship of our identities. By sharing firsthand accounts as counter narratives, we dismantle the expectations and misperceptions that other people place on who they think we are. Telling one's story creates opportunities to recognize the humanity in each other.

Exclude Euphemisms and Essentialization

Euphemisms are pervasive throughout teacher education. Euphemisms often function as code for inappropriate terms and expressions. The highly regarded *Oxford English Dictionary* (OED) defines this linguistic expression as "a less distasteful word or phrase used to substitute something harsher or more offensive." The word 'urban' is often used as a euphemism. Historically, urban means city, the opposite of country; not rural or a town, referring to the OED. However, in the absence of universal meaning, 'urban' has evolved to mean "settlement size, population density, or economic advancement" (Wineman et al., 2020, p. 254). In teacher education, the word 'urban' has become code for Black and Brown people living in underserved and under-resourced communities (Pryal, 2015). A Boolean search for the term 'inner-city' will yield academic papers using the referent to mean life in Black and Brown contexts.

In the same way that binary pronouns (e.g., she and he) are inappropriate for some people, the umbrella terms Black and AAPI do not apply to all people who appear Black or AAPI. The 'other-race effect' phenomenon "refers to the difficulty of discriminating between faces from ethnic and racial groups other than one's own" (Yang et al., 2018, p. 596) with the potential for misidentification and cultural bias. When referring to racial identity, Black denotes dark-skinned people descended from Africans who live across the African diaspora. When Black is paired with American, the referent is Black American or African American to mean people of African descent who are U.S. nationals. It is essential for teacher leaders and teacher educators to have accurate knowledge of colleagues' and students' racial and ethnic identity. The United States is home to millions of Black people born in the country and from other nations. Data from 2019 show that 4.6 million Black people living in the United States were born in Africa and the Caribbean (Tamir, 2021). Nigeria, Ethiopia, and Ghana rank among the highest African countries represented, with Jamaica, Haiti, and the Dominican Republic representing Caribbean nations (Anderson & López, 2018). While Black Americans may be more inclined to embrace their African heritage, African- and Caribbean-born immigrants distinguish themselves from Black Americans (Rahier & Hintzen, 2014).

> In a society that has equated all persons defined as [B]lack with inferiority and savagery . . . . it is not surprising that [B]lacks—from Africa, the Caribbean, and elsewhere—make it known that they were not one of "them" (Rahier & Hintzen, 2014, p. 194).

The terms 'Chinese' or 'Korean' are unsuitable catchalls for the millions of people of Asian descent living in the United States today. More than 30 separate ethnic groups representing East, South, and Southeast Asia reside in the United States (Kiang, n.d.). For some people, 'Asian' or 'Pan-Asian' referents are more tolerable, to the objectionable 'Oriental,' an adjective for a rug, carpet, and precious stones, with an obsolete application to geography, including *exotic* human beings (Li & Nicholson, 2021). The misidentification of the many Asian ethnicities in the United States contributes to a significant amount of the racism experienced by people of Asian descent. Much of the anti-Asian sentiment in the United States reveals the confusion of country of ancestry and current nationality. From World War II to the current COVID-19 pandemic, people of Asian origin who were born in the United States have been taunted as the enemy who should go back to China or their home country, viewed as "not-true Americans" (Iwamoto & Liu, 2010, p. 80). Essentialist identification practices must stop by recognizing that Chinese Americans comprise 23% of the Asian population or 5.4 million people in the United States, Filipinos representing 18% or 4.2 million, 2.2 million people with Vietnamese roots, of Korean lineage 1.9 million, and Japanese heritage 1.5 million (Budiman & Ruiz, 2021).

Navigate New Spaces

The sixth ABAR Orientation is navigating new spaces, for example, border crossing. Field experiences that situate students in unfamiliar settings for experiential learning are staples of teacher education. Crossing borders provides a physical transfer of bodies for an intellectual flow and exchange between different spaces (Droux & Hofstetter, 2014). The transfer and exchange are necessary given the reality of differing lived experiences, lenses, and points of view between learners, teachers, and administrators. Almost daily, in any public school in the United States the majority of future educators will enter classrooms where their formative years will most assuredly differ from those of the students they teach. The latest available demographic data of K–12 public school teachers comes from the 2017–2018

National Teacher and Principal Survey that shows 80% of U.S. teachers are White. Teacher candidates must learn to navigate new, sometimes unfamiliar spaces. It is incumbent for teacher educators to facilitate the process by which students navigate and make sense of their identities in that context.

Yet, crossing physical boundaries can evoke a "pedagogy of discomfort" that "invite[s] students and educators to examine how our modes of seeing [and navigating our worlds are] . . . shaped specifically by the dominant culture" (Boler, 1999, p. 179.). The residual of hate tends to develop from lack of authentic understanding about another human being. Yet, to paraphrase Howard's (2016) title, You Can't Teach Who or What You Don't Know. To maximize the benefit of navigating new spaces requires reflection on the written and physical border crossings that we discuss in the next section.

REFLECTION ON THE EFFECTIVENESS OF PRACTICE

Milner (2007) analyzes the intersection of race, culture, and researcher positionality to guide researchers in the process of racial and cultural consciousness to conduct education research. He frames his analysis, mindful of the seen, unseen, and unforeseen dangers of inquiry rooted in race and culture, through a framework of researcher racial and cultural positionality:

- Researching the self
- Researching the self with others
- Engaged reflection and representation
- Shifting from self to system.

In this section, we apply Milner's approach to research revealing knowledge about ourselves and others in higher education and educator preparation programs to the end of building a system and culture that embodies antiracist practice, individually and collectively.

Reflecting on Self

Look inward to investigate one's thoughts, emotions, decisions, and behaviors. Milner iterates the process of recognizing and responding to race and culture through a process that rejects the exploitation, misinterpretation, and misrepresentation of individuals and communities of color. We apply L.I.S.T.E.N. to reject narratives that distract and deflect authenticity and agency of others.

Learn Correct Names and Pronouns

- What do I know about my chosen and family names? How do I feel about them?

Implement Inclusive Leadership

- How do I define DEI? Where does my understanding fit on the accuracy scale?

Show Love (and Understanding)

- What is my knowledge of agapé love? How do I practice self-care?

Tell Your Story

- What is my origin story? What more would I like to know about my cultural identity?

Exclude Euphemisms

- How do I respond or react when I encounter racism? How might I be more culturally responsive?

Navigate New Spaces

- How comfortable am I in my own skin?

Reflecting on Self in Relation to Others

Investigate oneself in relation to communities and those who make up a community. Implicit here is recognizing the cultural contexts that make up a community that inform individual worldviews and personal narratives. Inherent within any community are issues of power that leverage self and collective interests, engagement, norms, and language within the community.

Learn Correct Names and Pronouns

- Who are the people in my environs? How might I learn their names, cultural background, and public identities?

Implement Inclusive Leadership

- How inclusive am I of the people and perspectives of students, staff, and colleagues in my practice? How do our differences and similarities enhance my work?

Show Love (and Understanding)

- Since kindness is an aspect of love, how would I rate the kindness that I extend to five students, five staff, and five colleagues by name? What shared characteristics do they have with you; each other?

Tell Your Story

- How does my existence in this country compare to the origin story of five different students, staff, and colleagues?

Exclude Euphemisms

- Where do code, pejorative, and racist terms appear in my lexicon? How do I respond or react when I encounter racism happening to other people?

Navigate New Spaces

- What are the cultural venues in my community? Which ones do I visit and not visit, and why?

Engaged Reflection and Representation

Milner describes researchers and participants engaging in the process of co-reflection to examine the impact of research on their community, with race and culture at the core. We apply a similar approach of pause and reflect to recognize what is taking shape with a community.

Learn Correct Names and Pronouns

- How do we refer to each other? When do we use our pedigree before our names? When do we encourage others to refer to us by our first name only?

Implement Inclusive Leadership

- How often are nonteaching staff included in initiatives to reexamine organizational culture? How do we address the implicit hierarchies and faculty privileges compared to that of staff?

Show Love (and Understanding)

- How do we define our culture as it currently exists? How do we reimagine culture as we would like it to exist?

Tell Your Story

- How do we recognize each other's contributions to the community?

Exclude Euphemisms

- What do we notice about verbal and nonverbal cues when communicating with each other?

Navigate New Spaces

- How can we cultivate a unified community rather than one with implicit hierarchies?

Shifting from Self to System: Examine Past and Present Institutional Norms

Here we engage in inquiry and examine issues from a broader institutional level to analyze policy issues that inform race and culture. Institutional history and knowledge of existing politics and policies inform how change and transformation have a future in the community, institution, or system.

Learn Correct Names and Pronouns

- How are students assigned to my classes? Who selects my advisees?

Implement Inclusive Leadership

- How do institutional norms inform work? Where does the institution permit me and others like me to be the face and voice of the institution?

Show Love (and Understanding)

- How does my workplace recognize or promote kindness?

Tell Your Story

- How does the institution recognize me and my culture?

Exclude Euphemisms

- How does the institution endorse or oppose charged language? How does the campus respond to rate and racism?

Navigate New Spaces

- How do I cross local and community borders? What does the institution do to facilitate border crossing?

MOVING FORWARD

As such, we assert that instructors who prefer to assign student nicknames instead of learning correct name pronunciations, teachers who require slavery reenactments, and White leaders who undermine colleagues of color operate from a place of ignorance. Racial stereotypes, bias, and falsehoods shroud the hate that often fosters anti-Black and anti-Asian racism. For this reason, mentors, guides, and even cooperating teachers play critical roles in helping future teachers to process their school-related encounters. One aim for writing this chapter is to speak truth to power that names our challenges, featuring our efforts to overcome them along with occasional accomplishments. Exposure to new perspectives through the curricula is an indirect opportunity to build empathy. Sharing our encounters in written form permits readers to capture a glimpse of our real-life circumstances. While students and colleagues bestow privilege on our positions, to begin to grasp the myriad oppressive situations that we encounter as women teacher-scholars, our words highlight the unavoidable steps beyond Du Bois's (1903) 'double consciousness' to a place where we straddle multiple worlds. Our unique situatedness gives us member and visitor status to experience "both from the outside in and from the inside out" (hooks, 1994, ix).

Moving forward, Drs. Davis and Hagiwara (the authors of this manuscript) have recently been appointed to increased leadership roles in their college. Added to her duties as Graduate Program coordinator, Dr. Davis now serves as interim deputy department chair. Dr. Hagiwara has been reassigned from serving as department chair to being appointed interim associate dean for Academic Affairs. We cannot ignore the historical significance of being appointed to these leadership positions. Moreover, Dr. Davis serves with another Black woman scholar serving as department chair; two Black women scholars are now leading the largest department in the second largest college on campus. Dr. Hagiwara is the second AAPI to serve as an academic associate dean in the college. Prior to her new appointment, Dr. Hagiwara was the first AAPI department chair in the college. Although temporary positions, we pay close attention to our positionalities among colleagues as we continue to work toward finding ways to meaningfully introduce and implement our ABAR Orientation—L.I.S.T.E.N.—to everyone engaged in teacher education.

NOTES

1. Although Black, Black American, and African American are nuanced in the academic literature, herein the terms are used interchangeably.

2. The *Summer of Racial Reckoning* refers to months of July and August in 2020 when people around the world expressed grief and anger in daily protests about racial injustice, primarily against African Americans. The unrest was in response to the death of George Floyd, caused when a Minneapolis police officer knelt on Floyd's neck for 9 min and 29 s.

REFERENCES

Adichie, N. C. (2009, July). The danger of a single story. [Video file]. https://www.ted.com/talks/chimamanda_ngozi_adichie_the_danger_of_a_single_story?utm_content=talk&utm_source=linkedin.com&utm_medium=referral&utm_term=social-science&utm_campaign=social

Aguirre, A., & Martinez, R. (2002). Leadership practices and diversity in higher education: Transitional and transformational frameworks. *Journal of Leadership Studies*, *8*(3), 53.

Alexander, G. R. (2021, June). *National Commission to address racism in nursing*. https://www.nursingworld.org/~49f737/globalassets/practiceandpolicy/workforce/commission-to-address-racism/final-defining-racism-june-2021.pdf

Alex-Assensoh, Y. (2017). What's love got to do with it? *Diverse Issues in Higher Education*, *34*(16), 24.

Anderson, M., & López, G. (2020, May 30). *Key facts about black immigrants in the U.S.* Pew Research Center. https://www.pewresearch.org/fact-tank/2018/01/24/key-facts-about-black-immigrants-in-the-u-s/

Bauer, G. R., Braimoh, J., Scheim, A. I., & Dharma, C. (2017). Transgender-inclusive measures of sex/gender for population surveys: Mixed-methods evaluation and recommendations. *PloS One*, *12*(5), e0178043. https://doi.org/10.1371/journal.pone.0178043

Bergey, B. W. (2021). The stereotype does not define us: The social influences and life experiences that led Asian American men to pursue a teaching career. *Teaching and Teacher Education*, *103*, 103352. https://doi.org/10.1016/j.tate.2021.103352

Boler, M. (1999). *Feeling power: Emotions and education*. Routledge.

Brennan, R. (2016, January 25). In efforts to boost teacher diversity, Asians and Pacific Islanders seek inclusion. *Education Week*. https://www.edweek.org/leadership/in-efforts-to-boost-teacher-diversity-asians-and-pacific-islanders-seek-inclusion/2016/01

Budiman, A., & Ruiz, N. G. (2021, May 16). *Asian Americans are the fastest-growing racial or ethnic group in the U.S.* Pew Research Center. https://www.pewresearch.org/fact-tank/2021/04/09/asian-americans-are-the-fastest-growing-racial-or-ethnic-group-in-the-u-s/

Chow, C. J. (2017). Teaching for social justice: (Post-) model minority moments. *Journal of Southeast Asian American Education and Advancement*, *12*, 2, Article 3. DOI: 10.7771/2153-8999.1155

Cochran, R. F. J., & Calo, Z. R. (2017). *Agape, justice, and law: How might Christian love shape law?*. Cambridge: Cambridge University Press.

D'amico, D., Pawlewicz, R. J., Earley, P. M., & McGeehan, A. P. (2017). Where are all the Black teachers? Discrimination in the teacher labor market. *Harvard Educational Review*, *87*(1), 26–49. https://doi.org/10.17763/1943-5045-87.1.26

Droux, J., & Hofstetter, R. (2014). Going international: The history of education stepping beyond borders. *Paedagogica Historica*, *50*(1/2), 1–9. https://doi-org.ezproxy.montclair.edu/10.1080/00309230.2013.877500

Du Bois, W. E. B., & Gibson, D. B. (1903). *The souls of Black folk*. Penguin Books.

Figlio, D. (2018, August 20). *The importance of a diverse teaching force*. Brookings. https://www.brookings.edu/research/the-importance-of-a-diverse-teaching-force/

Flagherty, C. (2021, February 17). What's really going on with respect to bias and teaching evals? (n.d.). https://www.insidehighered.com/news/2021/02/17/whats-really-going-respect-bias-and-teaching-evals

Giroux, H. (1993). Living dangerously: Identity politics and the new cultural racism-towards a critical pedagogy of representation. *Counterpoints*, *1*, 89–124. http://www.jstor.org/stable/45136433

Gitomer, D. H., Brown, T. L., & Bonett, J. (2011). Useful signal or unnecessary obstacle? the role of basic skills tests in teacher preparation. *Journal of Teacher Education*, *62*(5), 431–445. https://doi.org/10.1177/0022487111412785

Griffin, K., Bennett, J., & York, T. (2020). *Leveraging promising practices: Improving the recruitment, hiring, and retention of diverse & inclusive faculty*. Aspire: Institutional Change Initiative. https://doi.org/10.31219/osf.io/dq4rw

Hagedorn, L. S., Chi, W. Y., Cepeda, R. M., & McLain, M. (2007). An investigation of critical mass: The role of Latino representation in the success of urban community college students. *Research in Higher Education*, *48*, 73–91. https://doi.org/10.1007/s11162-006-9024-5

Harewood, A., & Keefer, T. (2009). Revolution as a new beginning. *Upping the Anti*, *2*. https://uppingtheanti.org/journal/article/02-revolution-as-a-new-beginning/

Hernandez, J. (2021). *Hate crimes reach the highest level in more than a decade*. NPR.org.

Herron, A. (2019, September 10). Middle school cancels 'slave ship' reenactment. *Indianapolis Star*. http://ezproxy.montclair.edu:2048/login?url=https://www-proquest-com.ezproxy.montclair.edu/newspapers/middle-school-cancels-slave-ship-reenactment/docview/2287326260/se-2?accountid=12536

hooks, b. (2018). *All about love: New visions*. Harper Perennial.

hooks, b. (1994). *Teaching to transgress: Education as the practice of freedom*. Routledge.

Howard, G. R. (2016). *We can't teach what we don't know: White teachers, multiracial schools*. Teachers College Press.

Iwamoto, D. K., & Liu, W. M. (2010). The impact of racial identity, ethnic identity, Asian values and race-related stress on Asian Americans and Asian international college students' psychological well-being. *Journal of Counseling Psychology*, *57*(1), 79–91. https://doi.org/10.1037/a0017393

Johnson, H. L. (2017). *Pipelines, pathways, and institutional leadership: An update on the status of women in higher education*. American Council on Education.

Kendi, I. X. (2020). *How to be an antiracist*. Btb.

Kiang, P. (n.d.). *Understanding our perceptions of Asian Americans*. Asia Society. https://asiasociety.org/education/understanding-our-perceptions-asian-americans

Kim, N. Y. (2016). Critical thoughts on Asian American assimilation in the whitening literature. In M. Zhou & A. C. Ocampo (Eds.), *Contemporary Asian America (third edition)* (pp. 554–575). New York University Press.

Kohli, R., & Solórzano, D. G. (2012). Teachers, please learn our names!: Racial microaggressions and the K-12 classroom. *Race Ethnicity and Education, 15*(4), 441–462. https://doi.org/10.1080/13613324.2012.674026

LaBue, A. C. (1960). Teacher certification in the United States: A brief history. *Journal of Teacher Education, 11*(2), 147–172. https://doi.org/10.1177/002248716001100203

Lee, E. (2015). *The making of Asian America: A history*. Simon & Schuster.

Li, Y., & Nicholson, H. L., Jr. (2021). When "model minorities" become "yellow peril"-Othering and the racialization of Asian Americans in the COVID-19 pandemic. *Sociology Compass, 15*(2), e12849. https://doi.org/10.1111/soc4.12849

MacNamara, J., Glann, S., & Durlak, P. (2017). Experiencing misgendered pronouns: A classroom activity to encourage empathy. *Teaching Sociology, 45*(3), 269–278. https://doi.org/10.1177/0092055X17708603

Marchiondo, L. A., Verney, S. P., & Venner, K. L. (2021). Academic leaders' diversity attitudes: Their role in predicting faculty support for institutional diversity. *Journal of Diversity in Higher Education*. Advance online publication. https://doi.org/10.1037/dhe0000333

Menakem, R. (2017). *My grandmother's hands*. Central Recovery Press.

Milner, H. (2007). Race, culture, and researcher positionality: Working through dangers seen, unseen, and unforeseen. *Educational Researcher, 36*(7), 388–400. http://www.jstor.org/stable/30136070

National Center for Education Statistics. (NCES). (2021). *The condition of education 2021: Public high school graduation rates*. Institute of Education Sciences. https://nces.ed.gov/programs/coe/indicator/coi

O'Meara, K. A., Culpepper, D., & Templeton, L. L. (2020). Nudging toward diversity: Applying behavioral design to faculty hiring. *Review of Educational Research, 90*(3), 311–348. https://doi.org/10.3102/0034654320914742

Pryal, K. R. G. (2015). Heller's scapegoats. *North Carolina Law Review, 93*, 1439–1474. https://ssrn.com/abstract=2606062

Rahier, J. M., & Hintzen, P. (2014). *Problematizing Blackness: Self ethnographies by Black immigrants to the United States*. Taylor & Francis.

Salganik, M. J., & Watts, D. J. (2008). Leading the Herd Astray: An experimental study of self-fulfilling prophecies in an artificial cultural market. *Social Psychology Quarterly, 74*(4), 338–355. https://doi.org/10.1177/019027250807100404

Schaeffer, K. (2021, December 14). *America's public school teachers are far less racially and ethnically diverse than their students*. Pew Research Center. https://www.pewresearch.org/fact-tank/2021/12/10/americas-public-school-teachers-are-far-less-racially-and-ethnically-diverse-than-their-students/#:~:text=About%20eight%2Din%2Dten%20U.S.,or%20Asian%20American%20(2%25)

Silverstein, J. (2021, June 4). The global impact of George Floyd: How Black Lives Matter protests shaped movements around the world. https://www.cbsnews.com/news/george-floyd-black-lives-matter-impact/

Stein S., de Andreotti V. O. (2016). Decolonization and higher education. In M. Peters (Ed.), *Encyclopedia of Educational Philosophy and Theory*. Springer. https://doi.org/10.1007/978-981-287-532-7_479-1

Tamir, C. (2021, August 4). *The growing diversity of black America*. Pew Research Center's Social & Demographic Trends Project. https://www.pewresearch.org/social-trends/2021/03/25/the-growing-diversity-of-black-america/

Truong, D. M., Tanaka, M. L., Cooper, J. M., Song, S., Talapatra, D., Arora, P., Fenning, P., McKenney, E., Williams, S., Stratton-Gadke, K., Jimerson, S. R., Pandes-Carter, L., Hulac, D., & García-Vázquez, E. (2021). School psychology unified call for deeper understanding, solidarity, and action to eradicate anti-AAAPI racism and violence. *School Psychology Review*, 50(2–3), 469–483. https://doi.org/10.1080/2372966X.2021.1949932

Turner, C. S. V., Gonzalez, J. C., & Wood, J. L. (2008). Faculty of color in academe: What 20 years of literature tell us. *Journal of Diversity in Higher Education*, 1(3), 159–168. https://doi.org/10.1037/a0012837

Villegas, A., & Davis, D. (2007). Approaches to diversifying the teaching force: Attending to issues of recruitment, preparation, and retention. *Teacher Education Quarterly*, 34(4), 137–147. http://www.jstor.org/stable/23479116

Wheeler, S. L. (2016). Two short "as" and a rolling "r": Autoethnographic reflections on a "difficult" name. *SAGE Open*, 6(3), 1–11. https://doi.org/10.1177/2158244016658935

Wineman, A., Yélognissè Alia, D., & Anderson, C. L. (2020). Definitions of "rural" and "urban" and understandings of economic transformation: Evidence from Tanzania. *Journal of Rural Studies*, 79, 54–268.

Yang, C.-T., Fifić, M., Chang, T.-Y., & Little, D. R. (2018). Systems factorial technology provides new insights on the other-race effect. *Psychonomic Bulletin & Review*, 25(2), 596–604. https://doi.org/10.3758/s13423-017-1305-9.

Yang, M. (2021). More than 9,000 anti-Asian incidents reported in US since pandemic started. *The Guardian*. https://www.theguardian.com/world/2021/aug/12/anti-asian-stop-aapi-hate-covid-report

Yellow Horse, A. J., Jeung, R., Lim, R., Tang, B., Im, M., Higashiyama, L. S., & Chen, M. (2021). *Stop AAPI hate national report*. https://stopaapihate.org/wp-content/uploads/2021/08/Stop-AAPI-Hate-National-Report-Final.pdf

Yi, J., & Todd, N. R. (2021). Internalized model minority myth among Asian Americans: Links to anti-Black attitudes and opposition to affirmative action. *Cultural Diversity and Ethnic Minority Psychology*, 27(4), 569–578. https://doi.org/10.1037/cdp0000448.

Chapter 4

Diversity, Equity, and Inclusion Matter

Preparing Teacher Candidates to Become Activist Educators

Benita R. Brooks, Ramona T. Pittman,
Jaime Coyne, Tori Hollas, and Mae Lane

Teacher Education Programs (TEPs) are struggling to prepare teacher candidates on how to use transformative pedagogies that benefit the educational outcomes of diverse students who have been disenfranchised across racial, economic, and linguistic lines. TEPs have a responsibility to prepare their teacher candidates with skills, knowledge, and practices in promoting diversity, equity, and inclusion (DEI), especially during a time of political and cultural unrest. In this chapter, we share qualitative data from a longitudinal study evaluating the effect of an innovative diversity certificate program in efforts to equip teacher candidates through engaging and inclusive practices. Several themes emerged, including the importance of incorporating inclusive practices and advocating for change, understanding the value of self-awareness, and promoting an equitable learning environment. We hope to inspire other TEPs to incorporate similar diversity programs that prepare teachers to work with students from diverse backgrounds.

INTRODUCTION

Literature supports the claim that TEPs are struggling to prepare teacher candidates to use transformative pedagogies that benefit the educational outcomes of Black, Indigenous, People of Color (BIPOC) students who have been "disenfranchised across racial, economic, and linguistic lines" (Allen et al., 2017, p. 2). In a recent article, Ladson-Billings (2021a) called on education scholars and researchers to rethink education and consider the pandemic as "an opportunity to reset education using a more robust and culturally centered pedagogy" (para 1). Yet, several states, including Texas, passed legislation forbidding any teachings that "challenge and complicate dominant narratives about the role of race in the country's history and identity" (Zao & Kao, 2021, para 1). This new legislation has complicated matters even more for TEPs, specifically those that train K–12 teachers to use research-based practices to "reflect on both the economic impact of systemic racism and on how their own biases may impact their interactions with students and families" (Metro, 2021, para 1). Because we come to this chapter as teacher educators with a range of K–12 teaching and research experiences, it is our collective belief that we move our future educators away from an educational space that ignores cultural histories and perspectives (Thomas, 2020) to a space that fosters innovative and inclusive practices that transform them to enact equitable practices as first-year teachers in the classroom. This chapter draws upon qualitative data from a longitudinal study that examines a diversity certificate program's effect on teacher candidates' preparedness to work as first-year teachers with diverse student populations.

One of the inspirations for the development of the program was the alarming fact that only one-third of our state's (Texas) principals perceive their first-year teachers as being well prepared to work both with a diverse student population and a diverse parent and school community population (TEA, 2019). We can imagine that other states across the nation have similar statistics, prioritizing the need for specialized training in this area for teacher candidates. Marchitello and Trinidad (2019) identified the following three key areas of focus to help schools of education and teacher preparation programs better prepare teacher candidates to serve students from diverse backgrounds: (a) conduct a comprehensive curricular review to incorporate diverse perspectives and experiences; (b) expose candidates to diverse settings, students, educators, and experiences across a variety of roles throughout their education and training; and (c) provide training on DEI for faculty members, staff, and students. Recently, Bukko and Liu (2021) recommended TEPs focus on utilizing equity-focused instruction and coaching to develop teachers' critical consciousness of the systems of power and privilege in educational institutions.

At our university, we provide teacher candidates with field experience opportunities to ensure they gain experience working in diverse settings. Contrarily, we have not conducted a comprehensive curricular review to ensure our undergraduate program reflects diverse perspectives and experiences. Currently, our teacher candidates are not required to take the one and only multicultural education course offered. As a result, we witnessed teacher candidates in our courses display a certain set of biases, stereotypes, preconceived notions, and prejudices. Research has indicated that it is the responsibility of the TEPs to dispel these predispositions and to prepare socially just educators "to navigate a system that often dehumanizes its students and teachers through high-stakes standardized measures of 'proficiency' and other such deficit-based practices" (Chaplin & Daoud, 2017, p. 15).

In response, the first author (Brooks) developed a diversity certificate program for K–12 teacher candidates. Currently, the DEI program, though highly encouraged, is not yet required for our teacher candidates. As co-coordinators of the 4+1 TEACH Program,[1] the third, fourth, and fifth authors (Coyne, Hollas, and Lane) examined how the diversity certificate program how teachers create an inclusive classroom environment. The 4+1 TEACH candidates were chosen for this program because they are working with a diverse student population.

It is evident that TEPs need to focus on the development of teacher candidates' dispositions and practices for equity and inclusion (Sandoval et al., 2020). Howard (2019) declared, teacher education as a field must be challenged, and teacher educators as actors in this field must "do better, teach better, challenge injustice better, and prepare teachers in an authentic way that recognizes racial realities, the persistence of racial injustice and the demographic realities of our current racial state" (p. viii). The purpose of this chapter is to examine a diversity certificate program's impact on teacher candidates' preparedness to work as first-year teachers with diverse student populations. In this chapter, we respond to Howard's (2019) call by describing an innovative diversity certificate program designed to equip teacher candidates with tools to disrupt educational systems and processes that perpetuate injustice and inequity in schools.

Further, in this chapter, we reflect on the ways the diversity certificate program fostered innovative and inclusive practices that transformed teacher candidates to enact equitable practices as first-year teachers in the classroom. Thus, we build on the scholarship that calls on TEPs to take the following steps: (a) present social justice in ways that allow candidates to understand how they can become change agents, (b) teach candidates to define social justice in terms of the realities faced by their students, and (c) help candidates use their expanding definition of social justice to challenge inequities and promote systemic change (Chaplin & Daoud, 2017).

THEORETICAL PERSPECTIVE

The theoretical underpinnings for this chapter focus on social judgment theory (Sherif, 2019) and critical race theory (CRT) (Howard, 2019) to examine the experiences of teacher candidates who participated in a DEI Undergraduate Certificate Program. A core premise of Sherif's (2019) social judgment theory is that when people are given a new piece of information, they automatically judge that content based on their current knowledge and experience. The new information is placed into one of three zones: (a) latitude of acceptance, (b) latitude of rejection, and (c) latitude of noncommitment (Griffin et al., 2019, p. 171). According to Sherif, our ego involvement on a certain topic is what leads us to place the information in the zones (Griffin et al., 2019). Ego involvement is described as how important a topic is to one's own life. In other words, ego involvement addressed the question: How important is it to us? For example, if someone countered a belief that had high ego involvement, the individual will be in the zone of rejection because they do not believe in what is stated. On the contrary, if someone stated a belief in the latitude of acceptance, then they agreed with what is stated. To shift a person's attitude, they must judge how far it is from their original belief. Once the thought process is complete, adjustments can be made based on the new information that is received. Sherif exclaimed the information that is received in the best way is the information that is far enough away from that anchored belief but still within the latitude of acceptance (Griffin et al., 2019).

CRT has become prevalent in the current news cycle, as several political figures, state and local governments, and school districts attack the tenants that underlie it. Many employers now require DEI training. Those who disagree with such training or approaches have disputed the premise that teachers and students need such knowledge. CRT, however, has been around for several decades. Although it derived from the legal field (Ladson-Billings, 1998), CRT found its way into the education field. Even so, 25 years later, in several states such as Texas, Tennessee, and Oklahoma, educators have limited understanding of teaching about racism (Education Week, 2021).

To fully grasp why teaching about racism poses problems for some, one must understand what antiracist pedagogy means. Blakeney (2011) defines antiracist pedagogy as a paradigm within critical theory that is designed to disrupt the impact of racism to create a just and equitable society. In most TEPs, teacher candidates generally take one course labeled something along the lines of Foundations of Multicultural Education or Race, Class, Culture, and Gender in the Classroom (Tatum, 2001) to learn about 'others.' However, these courses may not always teach preservice teachers about themselves and their power and privileges, as Lawrence and Tatum (1997) posit that many White adults have reflected little about what it means to belong to their own racial group. Further, in a study examining White-identified preservice teachers' views on antiracist pedagogy, St. Denis and Schick (2003) found that preservice teachers believe that race does not matter, everyone has equal opportunity, and through individual acts and good intention, one can secure innocence as well as superiority.

Additionally, many teacher candidates will enter classrooms in which supervising teachers may not have had any courses pertaining to DEI (Tatum, 2001). Research, however, has shown that minoritized students fall behind their counterparts in math and reading (National Assessment of Educational Progress, 2019) and are overidentified for suspension and expulsion (Fenning & Rose, 2007). When teachers do not understand DEI, they can hold unwelcoming views about students from varying races that differ from their race—we understand this practice as racism. When that happens, teachers who demonstrate racism will continually set low expectations for students (Cherng, 2017) due to their deficit views of the students (Terrill & Mark, 2000), which affects their academic performance. Teachers who are not knowledgeable about DEI practices also demonstrate racist teaching without knowingly doing so.

Kailan (2002) observed how teachers used covert racism in the classroom without realizing it. In the study, Kailan (2002) reported that teachers read books with stereotypes about the characters' race, and for example reprimanded a Black student for behavior that was displayed by her White counterpart. Furthermore, Shah and Coles (2020) found that it was difficult to change teacher candidates' ideology about race and that some just learn to talk-the-talk after taking courses geared toward DEI. This means that, while teachers may change their ideology, it does not necessarily mean that it will transmit to practice.

In a recent study, Wamsted (2021) identified simple ways teachers can self-monitor for implicit bias. He suggested that teachers monitor implicit bias by not only tracking big acts of discipline—detentions, referrals, and calls home, but also monitor bias when handling medium-level volume issues and inappropriate phone usage. In another study, Thompson (2021) recommended using a well-crafted equity survey to help teachers discover and plan how to meet students' needs. Our work, therefore, was not only about providing a DEI certificate program for teacher candidates but also ensuring that students were able to turn the information into actionable items in their own classrooms and school communities. Our hope was to help teachers imagine their classroom becoming "a site of activism for young people" (Kinloch et al., 2020, p. 7) and to prepare them to become transformative change agents who "foster equitable learning that supports students' creativities and justice engagements" (Kinloch et al., 2020, p. 7). Thus, the DEI certificate program requires participants to explore social identities, such as race, gender, and class, and examines how they communicate implicit bias or convey a deficit view based on stereotypes, assumptions, or original beliefs.

ANTIRACIST TEACHER EDUCATION PRACTICE(S) AND IMPLEMENTATION

In this section, we will report on a DEI certificate program that was implemented at our university. The DEI certificate program was designed to disrupt educational systems and processes that perpetuate injustice and inequity in schools. It was also designed to foster the skills educators need to implement inclusive and equitable practices in classrooms and other learning spaces. To receive a certificate, teacher candidates had to successfully complete six DEI-related workshops totaling 12 clock hours. The original design of the program aligned with a face-to-face model but was placed online when the pandemic happened. As a result, there were four face-to-face workshops and two online workshops, including a closing workshop where teacher candidates shared the effect of the program on their personal and professional lives. As presented in table 4.1, the first two workshops took place during the fall semester, and the other four took place during the spring. Participants completed this program the year prior to their first year of teaching.

METHODOLOGY

Tucker-Smith (2021) stresses that effective equity professional development is critical in emphasizing a growth mindset and it is essential to assess the effectiveness over time. With the purpose of determining the impact of the DEI program on participants and on their teaching practices during their first year of teaching, we engaged in basic qualitative research.

Table 4.1 DEI Program and Descriptions

Workshop	Description
Workshop 1: Foundations in Diversity, Equity, and Inclusion	Provided a foundation on the different aspects of diversity, equity, and inclusion
Workshop 2: Culturally Responsive Classroom Management Practices	Provided strategies that will help teacher candidates survive their first year as a classroom teacher
Workshop 3: Unconscious Bias	Provided strategies for classroom teachers to self-reflect and build relationships
Workshop 4: Cross-cultural Communications	Built on the previous workshop on unconscious bias to address effective strategies to communicate with teachers, students, parents, and administrators
Workshop 5: Gendered Languages	Encompassed appropriate vocabulary needed to use within the realm of education to promote an inclusive classroom environment. Included a panel discussion with K–12 school administrators
Workshop 6: Creating an Inclusive Classroom	Involved a conversation about how to implement what participants learned in the program into their classroom as first-year teachers

Table 4.2 Participants' Demographics (All Names Are Pseudonyms)

Participant	Gender	Race	Teaching Level	Content
Maxine	F	W	Middle	SS/ELAR
Maria	F	H	Elementary	SC
Henry	M	AA	Middle	ELAR
Jennifer	F	W	Elementary	SC
Rebecca	F	W	Middle	SS/ELAR
Robert	M	W	High	Agricultural
Elizabeth	F	AA	Middle	Math
Veronica	F	H	Elementary	SC
Sarah	F	W	Middle	ELAR
Allison	F	H	Elementary	SC

AA=African American; ELAR=English, Language Arts; F=Female; H=Hispanic; M=Male; SC=Self-Contained; SS=Social Studies; W=White.

Participants

Participants were recruited from an educator preparation program from a public university located in the southern part of the United States. There were 10 first-year teachers who participated in this study. As presented in table 4.2, four participants taught at the elementary level ranging from grades kindergarten through fifth grade, five taught at the intermediate level ranging from grades 6 to 8, and one participant taught at the secondary level in grades ranging from 9 to 12. Purposeful sampling was employed (Palinkas et al., 2015; Patton, 1990), and participants were chosen because they were members of the 4+1 TEACH program in which they complete a graduate internship (as a teacher of record) in lieu of student teaching. The 4+1 TEACH candidates were chosen for this program because they are working with a diverse student population and can be tracked for research purposes since they are part of the program for the first three years of their teaching.

Instruments

Survey

Participants were asked the following question in a post-survey during their second semester of teaching: *What tools and resources have you used in your teaching that you acquired during the training?* To gain an understanding of the participants' reasoning, responses were thematically coded (Glaser & Strauss, 1967). In employing surveys, we can better interpret participants' experiences and applications during their first year of teaching after participating in the DEI training (Merriam, 2009).

Table 4.3 Summary of Themes and Explanations

Themes	Explanation
Incorporating Inclusive Practices and Advocating for Change	Participants shared the importance of incorporating inclusive practices in their classroom as well as being a model for advocacy and social justice
Self-Awareness	Participants shared how they identified their own biases and cultivated critical consciousness
Promoting an Equitable Environment in an Unequitable Society and School System	Participants shared the importance of advocating for their students to create a more equitable learning experience

Data Analysis

It was important to evaluate the participants' responses to gain a better understanding of their reasoning and teaching application. Using thematic coding (Glaser & Strauss, 1967), several themes emerged as shared in the following sections. We have also included a summarized table of the themes below (see table 4.3). As Ladson-Billings (1998) stressed, storytelling is a component of CRT, and it was important for our participants to share their experiences.

FINDINGS AND DISCUSSIONS

Incorporating Inclusive Practices and Advocating for Change

The importance of incorporating inclusive practices, its impact on working with diverse students, and advocating for change were common themes among the participants' responses. It has been long argued that there is a disconnect between the curriculum and academic performance for marginalized students resulting in lower standardized test scores, higher dropout rates, and disciplinary problems (Walker & Hutchison, 2021). In her research spanning over 30 years, Ladson-Billings has documented Black students who were in classrooms of teachers who practiced culturally relevant pedagogy academically outperformed their peers (Ladson-Billings, 2021a), providing compelling evidence on the importance of teachers providing inclusive practices for all students.

In incorporating inclusive practices, one commonly debated topic of instruction across the nation is in incorporating diverse texts (Walker & Hutchison, 2021). Ladson-Billings (2021b) stresses the importance of being able to understand and comprehend diverse texts, specifically in a world that has been focused primarily on White supremacy. In addition, students need the opportunity to read text that mirrors their own life and culture (Clark & Fleming, 2019). As an example, Allison shared, "I worked to curate more diverse perspectives in our literature because I want students to be able to offer their unique perspectives." Using diverse literature helps students make connections, and it aids in comprehension because the text is familiar to their background, family, and or experience (Clark & Fleming, 2019). It also promotes active learning, as students are able to identify with text as well as a sense of belonging in their learning environment (Walker & Hutchison, 2021).

Through their incorporation of inclusive practices, participants also demonstrated their role as a model for advocacy and social justice. Possessing social-political consciousness is key for teachers to successfully implement inclusive practices, and the DEI program not only provided them with tools and skills to model to others how to think critically about sociopolitical issues but also to recognize them in barriers to equality for diverse students warranting the need for systemic change (Chaplin & Daoud, 2017; Jones & Donaldson, 2021). One participant shared, "The DEI program opened my eyes and helped me to recognize and challenge injustices to our society that directly and indirectly affect our students and society." Another participant, Mark shared, "I continuously shared with my students' key terms, examples, and experiences that outlined diversity, equity, and inclusion. Without this program, I would not have been equipped to give them this knowledge and showcase my celebration and sensitivity for diversity."

Also as a model for change, participants shared their understanding of their critical role as a change agent. As an example, Maxine shared, "It is important for my students to be socially aware of events that affect them and their society. They also need to know how to go about challenging inequalities they witness or face." Teaching through an antiracist lens, teachers help bring awareness to historic injustices in efforts to challenge inequalities to promote systematic change (Chaplin & Daoud, 2017).

Teacher preparation programs by large generally have one or two classes that focus on equity in schools (Sandoval et al., 2020) so it was critical that our DEI program prepared our candidates to challenge inequities and act as a change agent for others including their students.

Self-Awareness

Participants also shared the importance of self-awareness in identifying their own biases and cultivating critical consciousness. Hollins and Govan (2015) stress that becoming culturally competent teachers is ongoing as one is active in their process of self-awareness in their assumptions about values, biases, and behavior which are critical components. One participant, Rebecca, shared her personal experience.

I thought that I understood what many people go through and that I connected with them on meaningful levels. I now know that I never made the connections that I tried to make because I forgot one crucial thing. Not every trauma is the same. I have gone through poverty, homelessness, parents with substance abuse, and many more life-altering circumstances. I tried to lump myself with people and think that we went through the same thing. My thoughts were very far from the truth. I may have gone through poverty, but I never went through poverty as a person of color. When they speak about challenging things, I don't throw out my life's story and think it brings them comfort. When I feel like sharing enough to make a connection, I do, but in a way that doesn't diminish anything, anyone else is going through.

D'Angelo (2018) calls for individuals to challenge their own racial reality and acknowledge that their view of race is limited.

White fragility is a term coined by D'Angelo (2018) in her attempt to explain why White people are defensive when discussing racism. Hill et al. (2021) suggested that White fragility refers to racial stress that is caused when Whiteness is challenged, albeit "critical discussions of white privilege, racism, race-based discrimination, and racial prejudice" (p. 1812). Further, White people are fragile because of the racially privileged environment in which they live and their inability to feel comfortable discussing race (D'Angelo, 2018), while many do not even understand the privilege they have as being White (Frankenberg, 1993). Therefore, White people make statements such as they do not see color, they are not racist, and often do not agree with the term White supremacy (D'Angelo, 2018). She believes that other races may have prejudices against other races; however, in the United States, only White people have the collective social and institutional power and privilege over People of Color to be racist, whereas People of Color do not hold this power.

In education courses, it is critically important to understand White fragility because students enrolled in such courses will be responsible for educating diverse learners. Hines (2016) found that preservice principals minimized the importance of White privilege by making fragile responses to course readings. Furthermore, Evans-Winter and Hines (2020) analyzed how White undergraduate, preservice teachers resist antiracist, teacher preparation courses. Additionally, the authors' analysis revealed how acts of White fragility were used against them. If future principals and future teachers exhibit racial stress when discussing Whiteness, power, and privilege, this will impede their ability to develop antiracist praxis (Evans-Winter & Hines, 2020).

DEI professional development workshops aim to disrupt Whiteness in hopes of removing any racial stress from preservice teachers so that critical conversations can be held, which should improve their praxis while teaching diverse learners. In becoming an antiracist teacher, one must understand and confront the power and privilege the person possesses. When students encounter an antiracist teacher, they will know that the teacher does not believe in stereotypes about the students based upon their race; therefore, the teacher sets high expectations for *all* learners and does not view certain learners as less intelligent, thus creating deficit thinking (Valencia, 1997). As empowered leaders, teachers have the responsibility to disrupt injustice starting in the classroom.

Promoting an Equitable Environment in an Unequitable Society and School System

The educational system has historically left marginalized students behind (Ladson-Billings, 2018). Participants shared the importance of advocating and providing resources for their students in an attempt to provide a more equitable learning experience. One common practice found in many schools across the nation is ability grouping, also termed "tracking"; many researchers (Modica, 2015; Preis, 2020; Worthy, 2010) have argued that this practice leads to segregation of races and socioeconomic classes. In fact, as Worthy (2010) warns, students in higher-level ability classes are more likely to be taught by more experienced teachers and lower-level ability by less experienced teachers. This perpetuates the segregation of students and widens the academic gap for marginalized and non-marginalized students (Modica, 2015). One of our participants Allison shared, "I incorporate mixed ability grouping in my literacy instruction. This is important because every student brings their own unique voice and ability." As Ladson-Billings (2018) argues that social funding of race is demonstrated through teachers' ability grouping, in which the higher ability groupings are generally White and higher income. Ladson-Billings (1995) recommends that teachers instill a community of learners approach, instilling and maintaining high expectations for the whole class.

Like Allison, participants shared the importance of every student sharing their unique voice and contributions. Inclusive teachers recognize the importance of creating a community that fosters collaboration, familiarity (Ghosh, 2021), and a supportive environment conducive to setting the bar for the entire class. Rogoff (1994) stresses that this type of model builds students' abilities to coordinate, lead, and support others beyond the classroom as they work collaboratively in a noncompetitive environment promoting an authentic academic discourse (Ghosh, 2021).

Participants also learned that "equity" was not the same for every student as Elizabeth stated. DEI helped me understand that despite each student having their own struggles and strengths, they all needed/wanted different levels of help. "Equity" was introduced to me through DEI. Previously, I believed that if I provided everyone with the same help that would be enough. However, the reality is that it isn't because every student carries their own baggage. Some might need less or more help. As a teacher, it is my job to help them where they are to reach their potential.

Many argue that the opportunity gap between student groups is widening, despite educational reforms because it does not target the main issue which is inequality (Weller & Hinnant-Crawford, 2021; Ladson-Billings, 2018). Also present is the issue of unconscious racial bias by many school leaders and even teachers impacting marginalized students (Benson & Fiarman, 2020). As Elizabeth shared, teachers need to advocate for their students in an inequitable school system.

But this is also an example of how Ladson-Billings so eloquently describes "bridge-building quality" in teachers in which teachers meet the students where they are through scaffolding and making new connections (p. 104). This increases class community and inclusiveness and instills high expectations for students (Ladson-Billings, 2009).

MOVING FORWARD

TEPs programs have a responsibility to incorporate diversity training in their curriculum. With our participants, we were able to witness the impact the DEI program can have on teacher candidates as they embark on their journey as a classroom teacher. We realize that we have a longer road ahead, but it is our hope that other TEPs will also prioritize DEI initiatives to better prepare teachers in working with diverse student populations. We believe it is time for TEPs to respond boldly to Ladson-Billings's (2021a) call to reset post-pandemic pedagogy to include more culturally centered teaching practices.

NOTE

1. Teacher candidates chosen for the 4+1 TEACH program are chosen through a rigorous admission process the semester in the last year of their program. In lieu of student teaching, they are hired as an intern serving as a teacher of record in a Title I school and are supported with intense mentoring as well as professional development. As they are completing their internship, they are also acquiring graduate hours toward a graduate degree.

REFERENCES

Allen, A., Hancock, S., Starker-Glass, T., & Lewis, C. W. (2017). Mapping culturally relevant pedagogy into teacher education programs: A critical framework. *Teachers College Record, 119*(1), 1–26.

Benson, T., & Fiarman, S. (2020). *Unconscious bias in schools*. Harvard Education Press.

Blakeney, A. M. (2011). Antiracist pedagogy: Definition, theory, and professional development. *Journal of Curriculum and Pedagogy, 2*(1), 119–132. https://doi.org/10.1080/15505170.2005.10411532

Bukko, D., & Liu, K. (2021). Developing preservice teachers' equity consciousness and equity literacy. *Frontiers in Education, 6*, 1–11. https://doi.org/10.3389/feduc.2021.586708

Chaplin, M. S., & Daoud, A. M. (2017). The promise of equity: Preparing future teachers to be socially just educators. In E. Petchauer & L. Mawhinney (Eds.), *Teacher education across minority-serving institutions: Programs, policies, and social justice* (pp. 15–34). Rutgers University Press.

Cherng, H. Y. S. (2017). If they think I can: Teacher bias and youth of color expectations and achievement. *Social Science Research, 66*, 170–186. https://doi.org/10.1016/j.ssresearch.2017.04.001

Clark, A., & Fleming, J. (2019). "They almost become the teacher": Pre-K to third-grade teachers' experiences reading and discussing culturally relevant texts with their students. *Reading Horizons, 58*(3), 23–51.

D'Angelo, R. (2018). *White fragility: Why it's so hard for White people to talk about racism*. Beacon Press.

Education Week. (2021, July 26). *Map: Where critical race theory is under attack*. https://www.edweek.org/policy-politics/map-where-critical-race-theory-is-under-attack/2021/06

Evans-Winters, V. E., & Hines, D. E. (2020). Unmasking white fragility: How whiteness and white student resistance impacts anti-racist education. *Whiteness and Education, 5*(1), 1–16. https://doi.org/10.1080/23793406.2019.1675182

Fenning, P., & Rose, J. (2007). Overrepresentation of African American students in exclusionary discipline: The role of school policy. *Urban Education, 42*(6), 536–559. https://doi.org/10.1177/0042085907305039

Frankenberg, R. (1993). *White women, race matters: The social construction of whiteness*. Routledge.

Ghosh, A. (2021). Promoting student discourse in a linguistically diverse community-of-learners classroom. *InterActions: UCLA Journal of Education & Information Studies, 17*(1), 16–46.

Glaser, B., & Strauss, A. (1967). *The discovery of grounded theory*. Aldine.

Griffin, E. M., Ledbetter, A., & Sparks, G. (2019). *A first look at communication theory* (10th ed.). McGraw-Hill.

Hill, T., Mannheimer, A., & Roos, J. M. (2021). Measuring White fragility. *Social Science Quarterly, 102*(4), 1812–1829.

Hines, III, M. T. (2016). The embeddedness of White fragility within White preservice principals' reflections on white privilege. *Critical Questions in Education, 7*(2), 130–145.

Hollins, C., & Govan, I. (2015). *Diversity, equity, and inclusion: Strategies for facilitating conversations on race.* Rowman & Littlefield.

Howard, T. C. (2019). Foreword. In K. T. Han & J. Laughter (Eds.), *Critical race theory in teacher education: Informing classroom culture and practice* (pp. vii–ix). Teachers College Press.

Jones, B., & Donaldson, M. (2021). Preservice science teachers' sociopolitical consciousness: Analyzing descriptions of culturally relevant science teaching and students. *Science Education, 106*(1), 3–26. https://doi-org.ezproxy.shsu.edu/10.1002/sce.21683

Kailan, J. (2002). *Antiracist education: From theory to practice.* Rowman & Littlefield.

Kinloch, V., Burkhead, T., & Penn, C. (2020). *Race, justice, and activism in literacy instruction.* Teachers College Press.

Ladson-Billings, G. (1995). Toward a theory of culturally relevant pedagogy. *American Educational Research Journal, 32*(3), 465–491. https://doi.org/10.3102/00028312032003465

Ladson-Billings, G. (1998). Just what is critical race theory and what's it doing in a nice field like education. *International Journal of Qualitative Studies in Education, 11*(1), 7–24. https://doi.org/10.1080/095183998236863

Ladson-Billings, G. (2009). *The Dreamkeepers: Successful teachers of African-American children.* Jossey-Bass.

Ladson-Billings, G. (2018). The social funding of race: The role of schooling. *Peabody Journal of Education, 93*(1), 90–105. https://doi.org/10.1080/0161956X.2017.1403182

Ladson-Billings, G. (2021a). I'm here for the hard re-set: Post pandemic pedagogy to preserve our culture. *Equity & Excellence in Education, 54*(1), 68–78. https://doi.org/10.1080/10665684.2020.1863883

Ladson-Billings, G. (2021b). I read you, but do you read me? Culturally responsive literacy teaching and learning. *Literacy Today, 38*(5), 20–22.

Lawrence, S. M., & Tatum, B. D. (1997). White educators' allies: Moving from awareness to action. In M. Fine, L. Weiss, L. Powell, & M. Wong (Eds.), *Off-White: Readings on race, power, and society* (pp. 333–342). Routledge.

Marchitello, M., & Trinidad, J. (2019, March). Preparing teachers for diverse schools: Lessons from minority serving institutions. *Bellwether Education Partners.* https://bellwethereducation.org/sites/default/files/Preparing%20Teachers%20for%20Diverse%20Schools_Bellwether.pdf

Merriam, S. B. (2009). *Qualitative research: A guide to design and implementation.* Jossey-Bass.

Metro, R. (2021, July). Outlawing best practices. *Inside Higher Education.* https://www.insidehighered.com/views/2021/07/20/faculty-member-confronts-challenges-training-k-12-teachers-about-racial-issues

Modica, M. (2015). "My skin color stops me from leading": Tracking, identity, and student dynamics in a racially mixed school. *International Journal of Multicultural Education, 17*(3), 76–90. https://doi.org/10.18251/ijme.v17i3.1030

National Assessment of Educational Progress. (NAEP). (2019). The nation's report card: Reading. National Center for Educational Statistics.

Palinkas, L., Horwitz, S., Green, C., Wisdom, J., Duan, N., & Hoagwood, K. (2015). Purposeful sampling for qualitative data collection and analysis in mixed method implementation research. *Administration and Policy in Mental Health, 42*(5), 533–544. https://doi.org/10.1007/s10488-013-0528-y

Patton, M. (1990). *Qualitative evaluation and research methods* (2nd ed.). Sage.

Preis, D. (2020). Preparing suburban school leaders to recognize everyday narratives that promote opportunity gaps. *Journal of Educational Leadership and Policy Studies, 4*(1), 1–24.

Rogoff, B. (1994). Developing understanding of the idea of communities of learners. *Mind, Culture, and Activity, 1*(4), 209–229.

Sandoval, C., van Es, E., Campbell, S. L., & Santagata, R. (2020). Creating coherence in teacher preparation: Examining teacher candidates' conceptualizations and practices for equity. *Teacher Education Quarterly, 47*(4), 8–32. link.gale.com/apps/doc/A639054766/AONE?

Shah, N., & Coles, J. A. (2020). Preparing teachers to notice race in classrooms: Contextualizing the competencies of preservice teachers with antiracist inclinations. *Journal of Teacher Education, 71*(5), 584–599. https://doi.org/10.1177/0022487119900204

Sherif, M. (2019). Social judgment theory. In E. M. Griffin, A. Ledbetter, & G. Sparks (Eds.), *A first look at communication theory* (10th ed., pp. 171–181). McGraw-Hill.

St. Denis, V., & Schick, C. (2003). What makes antiracist pedagogy in teacher education difficult? Three popular ideological assumptions. *The Alberta Journal of Educational Research, 49*(1), 55–69.

Taie, S., Goldring, R., & Spiegelman, M. (2017). *Characteristics of public elementary and secondary school teachers in the United States*. National Center for Education Statistics (NCES). U.S. Department of Education. In National Teacher and Principal Survey 2015–16. https://nces.ed.gov/pubsearch/pubsinfo.asp?pubid=2017072

Tatum, B. D. (2001). Professional development: An important partner in antiracist teacher education. In S. H. King & L. A. Castenell (Eds.), *Racism and racial inequality: Implications for teacher educators* (pp. 51–58). American Association of Colleges for Teacher Education.

Terrill, M. M., & Mark, D. L. (2000). Preservice teachers' expectations for schools with children of color and second-language learners. *Journal of Teacher Education, 51*(2), 149–155.

Texas Education Agency (TEA). (2019). *Educator preparation program candidate exit survey*. http://www.tea.state.tx.us/index2.aspx?id=2147485421&menu_id=2147483671

Thomas, D. (2020). One love, one heart. In V. Kinloch, T. Burkhead, & C. Penn (Eds.), *Race, justice, and activism in literacy instruction* (pp. 111–130). Teachers College Press.

Thompson, V. (2021, July 29). *Beginning the year with an equity survey.* Edutopia. https://www.edutopia.org/article/beginning-year-equity-survey

Tucker-Smith, N. (2021). The illusion of equity PD. *Educational Leadership, 78*(6), 72–75.

Valencia, R. R. (Ed.). (1997). *The evolution of deficit thinking: Educational thought and practice.* The Falmer Press.

Walker, S., & Hutchison, L. (2021). Using culturally relevant pedagogy to influence literacy achievement for middle school black male students. *Journal of Adolescent & Adult Literacy, 64*(4), 421–429. https://doi.org/10.1002/jaal.1114

Wamsted, J. (2021, January 22). *A simple way to self-monitor for bias.* Edutopia. https://www.edutopia.org/article/simple-way-self-monitor-bias

Weller, J., & Hinnant-Crawford, B. (2021). School leadership team competence for implementing equity systems change: An exploratory study. *The Urban Review, 53*(2), 1–19. https://doi.org/10.1177/0021886397332009

Worthy, J. (2010). Only the names have been changed: Ability groups revisited. *Urban Review, 42*(4), 271–295.

Zao, I., & Kao, J. (2021, August). Texas teachers say GOP's new social studies law will hinder how an entire generation understands race, history, and current events. *Texas Tribune.* https://www.texastribune.org/2021/08/03/texas-critical-race-theory-social-studies-teachers/

Chapter 5

Making Space for Critical Thought amid State Prohibitions

Critical Race Theory as a Framework to Inform Course Design and Student Learning Objectives

Marisol Diaz, Sarah M. Straub,
Tonya D. Jeffery, and Brian Uriegas

The recent emergence of focus on critical race theory (CRT) has created controversy in many areas, including the field of education. Legislation in states like Texas has resulted in increased restrictions on curriculum and placed increased limitations on classroom teachers. For preservice teachers, the ability to provide high-quality instruction for all students rests on a critical understanding of their lessons and pedagogical approaches to provide accurate and rigorous material to students. This chapter reimagines the *field experience* for PK–6 preservice teachers by focusing on program learning objectives (PLOs) and student learning objectives (SLOs), formal and informal assignments, and lesson planning, first examining the concepts of CRT and the implications it presents in the school setting, along with antiracist teaching practices and strategies. The chapter then shifts into a thorough explanation of the reimagined *field experience* that includes a framework for teacher preparation programs. The framework presents specific program and learning objectives (PLOs and SLOs) along with the correlating assignments that imbed CRT perspectives. The goal of this reimagined approach to the *field experience* component of the educator preparation program is an attempt to use a transformative approach to imagine and create a space where the work of educators can exist amid an oppressive system and promote social-justice-oriented practices by using critical theoretical frameworks to inform their current and future practices.

INTRODUCTION

Critical race theory (CRT), once a term rarely heard in mainstream U.S. society, has suddenly become part of the dominant discourse. The first time the term received such massive attention outside of academic circles was in early September 2020 when former president Donald Trump issued an executive order banning CRT from being used in government-sponsored training (Vought, 2020). The politicization of CRT has revealed the deep racial tensions and White supremacist ideologies existing in the United States and, in turn, brought forth the same existing tensions within the education system. For example, many states have banned the use of CRT in K–12 schools or other state-sponsored use. It is important to note, however, that CRT is often misportrayed in the political arena. It is not taught at the K–12 level and is, in fact, something almost exclusively reserved for higher education courses. Such assaults on education are a direct threat to academic rigor and set a precedent for the future of the education system itself.

Preparing future teachers to think critically about their role in society is imperative in the journey toward social justice. However, most teacher preparation curricula in higher education are void of critical perspectives. For example, our current university's PLOs do not include critical perspectives relevant to pedagogy, history, and oppression that directly impact schooling practices. Further, our PLOs cannot be altered or removed from courses and can create difficulties in systematically guiding preservice teachers toward more critical understandings of education.

To combat the perpetuation of hegemonic PLOs, we collaborated to reimagine their field experience courses and SLOs that explicitly align with the tenets of CRT. In this context, *field experiences* are courses preservice teachers are required to complete in order to apply their theoretical knowledge and skills to practice in the PK–6 school setting before earning a teaching degree. Therefore, this chapter will focus on how our work creates SLOs while maintaining PLOs. The chapter begins with a grounding in relevant CRT theoretical perspectives used to inform the creation of SLOs of preservice teachers in a field-based course. Next, it will continue with specific examples of the SLOs, and finally with recommendations for moving forward.

THEORETICAL PERSPECTIVES

Critical Race Theory

CRT originated from legal studies and drew from critical theory to create a framework centered on racism and declared that racism was embedded and maintained through the law (Delgado et al., 2017). Contrary to what is believed today, CRT did not come from educational theories but instead was brought to education, as some educational scholars saw its relevance and use in explaining racism in the educational system (Ladson-Billings & Tate, 1995). Further, misinformation concerning CRT is the incorrect view that K–12 teachers are teaching CRT in classrooms. To be clear, CRT is not taught as a core subject in K–12 schools. That is, K–12 school teachers do not teach CRT in the classroom as an academic topic. This kind of misinformation has fueled heated debates among teachers, parents, school administrators, and society.

CRT is more commonly used in critical academic educational spaces. CRT education scholars have used CRT as a lens to analyze racism in schooling (Ladson-Billings & Tate, 1995), teacher preparation programs (Solorzano & Bernal, 2001), and further theorize on the role of education itself (Brayboy, 2005; Solorzano & Yosso, 2020). CRT educational scholars view the school curriculum as a reflection of White supremacy (Delgado et al., 2017) and use CRT's defining qualities to examine the broader power structure's seemingly objective and neutral position on racism (Zamudio et al., 2011). CRT scholars believe that politics and mainstream political parties, including the "functioning of agencies like the education system itself, are actively implicated in maintaining and extending the grip that White people have on the major sources of power in 'Western' capitalist societies" (Gillborn, 2009, p. 497).

CRT is also a helpful framework that can deconstruct structural determinism and racialization in public schools. As one of its central tenets, CRT expresses "skepticism toward dominant legal claims of neutrality, objectivity, color blindness, and meritocracy" and larger power structures like government (Matsuda et al., 1993, p. 6). Therefore, CRT is a tool to critically analyze systemic issues of racism in education.

CRT in Schools

The tenets of CRT can be used to deconstruct structural determinism and racialization in public schools. In educational establishments, CRT maintains that racism is structural, and biased knowledge is disseminated through the curriculum. "Critical race theory sees the official school curriculum as a culturally specific artifact designed to maintain a White supremacist master script" (Ladson-Billings, 1995, p. 18). The following are some of the central tenets of CRT that are valuable tools to use as a critical analysis. CRT

- recognizes that racism is endemic to the United States;
- expresses skepticism toward dominant legal claims of neutrality, objectivity, color blindness, and meritocracy;

- challenges historicism and insists on a contextual/historical analysis of the law;
- insists on recognizing the experiential knowledge of People of Color and our communities of origin in analyzing law and society;
- is interdisciplinary and eclectic;
- works toward the end of eliminating racial oppression as part of the broader goal of ending all forms of oppression.

CRT's tenets express skepticism toward the ruling power's claims of neutrality and see racism and oppression as structurally and purposely designed (Delgado et al., 2017). The mainstream Western school curriculum is an artifact of White supremacist ideologies and structurally designed through a White supremacist lens to oppress and control society (Gillborn, 2009; Leonardo, 2004). Schools play an essential role in the socialization process of a society.

Using CRT as a theoretical framework can guide pedagogical practices that seek and encourage transformative thinking in students, especially future educators. Teachers are at the forefront of this imperative and can promote transformation in the classroom. Keeping theoretical frameworks like CRT in an educator's repertoire guides the teacher's thinking and practices. In order to combat a curriculum that oppresses and further marginalizes, pedagogical approaches must be critical and epistemological (Steinberg & Kincheloe, 2010). However, as mentioned earlier, the mainstream curriculum in schools is uncritical, racist, and biased—it prioritizes a dominant White society (Ladson-Billings, 1995).

Therefore, ensuring that teacher candidates clearly understand the effect of power and race in students' educational experiences is essential. Future educators need the academic understanding and rigor about these social and political issues and a holistic understanding of the historical racist and colonial past on which this country was founded. This affects a teacher's selection of materials, perceptions of students' capabilities, and views about the border school community.

ANTIRACIST AND CULTURALLY RESPONSIVE TEACHER EDUCATION PRACTICES

The field of education draws from many disciplines to inform best teaching practices. This multidisciplinary characteristic of education was used in the creation of SLOs as well. CRT helped ground the centrality of racism and pulled from antiracist teacher practices and culturally responsive tools to create meaningful SLOs. Most public school teachers feel disenfranchised and disconnected from their students and communities (Gause, 2008). Teachers are not even seen as researchers but are called practitioners and are often disconnected from the very field they engage in (Kincheloe, 2003).

According to Gay (2002), culturally responsive teaching benefits all students' academic achievement, social critique and consciousness, and individual self-worth. Culturally relevant education focuses on researching cultural issues related to science learning, teaching, curriculum, assessment/ evaluation, and teacher education. Education is culturally biased and comes from culturally maintained sources (Nieto, 2010). Preservice teachers would benefit from exploring socioeconomic, institutional, and cultural issues that influence teaching and learning.

Obtaining a critical education in this present century (i.e., 21st century) is more complicated than in the 20th century because of the negotiation and influence of power, politics, and the control that popular culture has over society (Gause, 2008). Gause (2008) views the current role of schools as a place where knowledge is transmitted based on how those in power define it. That is why CRT may help foster transformative critical thinking in preservice teachers (Gause, 2008). Teachers' knowledge about racism and power must extend beyond mere tolerance, awareness, and recognition that ethnic groups have different values and express them in multiple ways (Gay, 2002). Understanding how the mind functions in relation to culture, institutional, and historical contexts is a process that must be viewed holistically and not in separate disciplinary sections (Wertsch, 1998).

Using CRT and PLOs to Inform SLOs

Like many critical educators, working in the current White supremacist system while striving for social justice is more than challenging. However, we have found ways to continue our work without compromising our consciousness and ethical principles. This requires creativity and an ability to work within the system's framework. In our case, we used the existing program's learning outcomes to derive the SLOs informed by a CRT framework.

In the following section, we present five PLOs of the field experience course. In this course, teacher candidates are placed in PK–6 public schools during a 16-week long semester. Field experience courses are designed to help the teacher candidate apply their knowledge and skills and connect theory to practice in the public school. The following are the current PLOs of our program:

- **PLO 1.** Candidates know, understand, and use the major concepts, principles, theories, and research related to the development of children and

young adolescents to construct learning opportunities that support individual students' development, acquisition of knowledge, and motivation.
- **PLO 2.** Candidates know, understand, and demonstrate a high level of competence in the content areas of English language arts, mathematics, science, and social studies.
- **PLO 3.** Candidates use their knowledge of students, learning, curriculum, environment, diversity, communication, and community to plan and implement collaborative engaging, thought-provoking, inquiry-based instruction to meet the needs of all learners.
- **PLO 4.** Candidates know, understand, and use formal and informal assessment strategies to plan, evaluate, and strengthen instruction to promote the continuous intellectual, social, emotional, and physical development of all children.
- **PLO 5.** Candidates know, implement, evaluate, and reflect upon research-based teaching, professional ethics, and professional learning resources to establish and maintain positive, collaborative relationships with families, colleagues, professional organizations, and community agencies to promote the intellectual, social, emotional, physical growth, and well-being of all children.

Table 5.1 is used to capture PLOs, SLOs, and CRT tenets. The table includes simplified language for both the PLOs and the tenets of CRT. Moreover, it demonstrates that there are multiple opportunities and pathways to weave CRT into the existing curriculum by creating CRT-informed SLOs. CRT understands that racism is structural and embedded in most mainstream curriculum, including higher education (Sawchuk, 2021). Across the top of the table are the PLOs, and running perpendicularly are the tenets of CRT. At the center of the table is our conceptualization of how we embed CRT in our course through SLOs. Following the table is a description of each of the SLOs.

We developed new SLOs using CRT as a theoretical framework to inform our field courses. Included in each student's learning objectives is an assignment used to demonstrate the attainment of the learning objective. The student learning outcomes will be expanded upon in the following section, where we will describe the assignments that we plan to develop, which are intentionally grounded in from a CRT perspective.

SLO 1: Preservice Teachers Identify Critical Theories That Inform Best Teaching Practices for Diverse Students

Assignment. Critical Theories Annotated Bibliography. Preservice teachers will be introduced to critical learning theories such as Critical

Table 5.1 Opportunities for PLO and CRT Alignment

	PLO 1: Use of learning theories to support practices	PLO 2: Content knowledge	PLO 3: Inquiry-based instruction generated through knowledge of community	PLO 4: Formal and informal assessment strategies	PLO 5: Reflection on research-based teaching, professional ethics, etc.
CRT 1: Racism is endemic to the United States	Preservice teachers identify critical theories that inform best teaching practices for diverse students	Preservice teachers demonstrate their knowledge of best teaching practices through a critical lesson plan	Preservice teachers will explain the historical, socioeconomic, and cultural capital of their school and evaluate their possible effects on teaching and learning	Preservice teachers will evaluate their field placement classrooms through an antibias critical lens	Preservice teachers analyze ways their identity may influence their teaching
CRT 2: Skepticism about claims of neutrality, color blindness, meritocracy	Preservice teachers analyze ways their identity may influence their teaching	Preservice teachers demonstrate their knowledge of best teaching practices through a critical lesson plan			
CRT 3: Challenge ahistoricism; push for contextual history	Preservice teachers demonstrate their knowledge of best teaching practices through a critical lesson plan		Preservice teachers demonstrate their knowledge of best teaching practices through a critical lesson plan		Preservice teachers will explain the historical, socioeconomic, and cultural capital of their school and evaluate their possible effects on teaching and learning

(Continued)

74 Marisol Diaz, et al.

Table 5.1 (Continued)

	PLO 1: Use of learning theories to support practices	PLO 2: Content knowledge	PLO 3: Inquiry-based instruction generated through knowledge of community	PLO 4: Formal and informal assessment strategies	PLO 5: Reflection on research-based teaching, professional ethics, etc.
CRT 4: Experiential knowledge of People of Color (POCs)					
CRT 5: Interdisciplinary and eclectic	Preservice teachers demonstrate their knowledge of best teaching practices through a critical lesson plan				
CRT 6: Work to eliminate racial oppression, and ultimately all forms of oppression	Preservice teachers demonstrate their knowledge of best teaching practices through a critical lesson plan			Preservice teachers will evaluate their field placement classrooms through an antibias critical lens	

Note. The CRT tenets that we have selected are not an exhaustive list.

Pedagogy (Duncan-Andrade & Morrell, 2008), Culturally Responsive Pedagogy (Gay, 2002), and CRT (Ladson-Billings, 1995) and generate an annotated bibliography associated with these critical learning theories. The annotated bibliography must contain 10 sources that explore how a student's race/identity affects their schooling experiences. Preservice teachers use data to demonstrate correlations about how their interpretation of these critical learning theories impact K–12 students' learning experiences.

SLO 2: Preservice Teachers Analyze Ways Their Identity May Influence Their Teaching

Assignment. Positionality Critical Reflection Paper. Using a biased test and critical reflection from classroom readings, discussions, field experiences, and documentaries, preservice teachers will write a critical reflection on ways their positionality may influence their teaching.

SLO 3: Preservice Teachers Will Evaluate Their Field Placement Classrooms through an Antibias Critical Lens

Assignment. Anti-Bias Classroom Observation Checklist and Environmental Observation. Preservice teachers will engage in an environmental evaluation of their classrooms through an antibias lens addressing PLOs 3 and 5 as well as CRTs 1, 2, and 6. This assignment is supported by an adapted Preparing Early Childhood Professionals for Inclusion Anti-Bias Classroom Observation Checklist and Environmental Observation forms from Derman-Sparks et al. (2010). This checklist allows preservice teachers to evaluate images, books, classroom materials, and staff interactions through a binary Yes/No metric. Then, the preservice teachers will have the chance to critically evaluate their space, draw conclusions, and make recommendations. There are four rubrics and one reflection.

SLO 4: Preservice Teachers Demonstrate Their Knowledge of Best Teaching Practices through a Critical Lesson Plan

Assignment. Counterstory Lesson Plans. Preservice teachers will build upon their community analysis study to select a lesson to be taught in their placement. Preservice teachers will present multiple perspectives from historically marginalized groups. For example, preservice teachers will integrate social justice standards into their lesson plans and rationalize the connection and importance of the standard.

SLO 5: Preservice Teachers Will Explain Their School's Historical, Socioeconomic, and Cultural Capital and Evaluate Their Possible Effects on Teaching and Learning

Assignment. Critical Community Analysis Study. Utilizing research from the Annotated Bibliography project, class readings, and discussions, preservice teachers will create a presentation of their school community. Preservice teachers will focus on the communities' cultural capital (Bourdieu, 1986; Yosso, 2005), history, and an analysis of the socioeconomic makeup and explain their influence on their students and schools.

Each of the five SLOs is an effort to lead preservice teachers into a critical consciousness about their roles in society. Assignments alone are not enough to invite preservice teachers into a deeper understanding of racism and the nature of oppression. Engaging in critical thinking is a process and carries an agenda of transformational change that "brings together multiple beliefs about human understanding and misunderstanding, the nature of change, and the role of critique and education in society" (Freeman & Vasconcelos, 2010, p. 7). Preservice teachers should learn how to take a critical position when developing and implementing the curriculum and have the skills necessary to critically examine the implications of the subject matter that is taught (Kliebard, 1989). In so doing, preservice teachers can effectively teach diverse students and begin to unpack relevant components to the learner's history and ways of knowing.

MOVING FORWARD

Educators live in a world where their profession is reduced to teaching as a technical process, one that involves very little thought and creativity, and more submission and obedience to hierarchical educational structures, such as school administration and educational rhetoric (Apple, 1979; Kincheloe, 2003). This is mainly because the teaching profession has been influenced by Western industrial ideas of work that hold teachers as blue-collar workers who take orders from experts (Kincheloe, 2003). Additionally, teacher preparation programs are also influenced by such ideas that deskill educators and promote them not to think for themselves or be self-directed (Freeman & Vasconcelos, 2010).

Further, educational programs and commercial education materials, which delineate prescriptive pedagogical approaches and content, have been used to supplant teacher-created lessons. This acts to further suppress teaching styles where the teacher is reduced to playing a role and becomes a passive consumer of such materials (Villa, 2010). This has been shown to affect how preservice teachers think about and are involved in their teaching.

Additionally, educational programs have been called the 'deskilling' of teachers and can negatively affect both the student and the teacher, resulting in a poorer educational experience for both (Apple, 1979; Shannon, 1987). Critical reflection is vital in learning and meaning-making in the practice of teaching (Loughran, 2002). However, there is often little time for preservice teachers to reflect on their learning and practice. Moreover, preservice teachers are socialized from the beginning of their learning career to fit the traditional teaching canon of pre-packed and homogenized information.

The overwhelming majority of teachers are still White middle-class women (National Center for Education Statistics, 2021; Sleeter, 2008), and this trend is predicted to continue. At the same time, the K–12 student population is growing increasingly culturally and linguistically diverse (U.S. Department of Education, 2017). Preparing future educators to teach in socially just ways is crucial to a thriving democratic society. As professors, we understand the need to ensure that preservice teachers know about their positionality, have a holistic view of history, and their broader role in society. As professors in higher education institutions, we can sometimes accomplish and maintain oppressive structures, such as racism. Therefore, we embrace our ethical responsibility to do our part in dismantling hegemonic practices that maintain White supremacy.

The transformative approach to redesigning the field experience course that we propose in this chapter is the first of many steps in reimagining the teacher education curriculum through the critical lens of social justice. Ultimately, we understand that mere knowledge of racism will not end it. However, we hope that preservice teachers use these critical theoretical frameworks to inform their current and future practice. We also hope that by sharing this CRT-informed lens with our students, they will filter their observations in the field. SLOs attempt to imagine and create a space where our work can exist amid an oppressive system and promote social-justice-oriented practices. We conclude by sharing that this process of planning for our field-based courses through a critical race theoretical lens is personal to us and our unique location. Our desire is that readers will be motivated by the thought processes we have shared. Even in an oppressive system, there are ways to create spaces of resistance in the path toward transformation. This can result in revolutionary ideas in multiple field courses and, ultimately, a cultural shift in how we prepare our preservice teachers.

REFERENCES

Apple, M. (1979). *Ideology and curriculum*. Routledge & K. Paul.

Bourdieu, P. (1986). The forms of capital. In J. G. Robinson (Ed.), *Handbook of theory and research for the sociology of education* (pp. 241–258). Greenwood Press.

Brayboy, B. M. J. (2005). Toward a tribal critical race theory in education. *Urban Review, 37*(5), 425–446. https://doi.org/10.1007/s11256-005-0018-y

Delgado, R., Stefancic, J., & Harris, A. (2017). *Critical race theory: An introduction* (3rd ed.). NYU Press.

Derman-Sparks, L., Edwards, J. O., & National Association for the Education of Young Children. (2010). *Anti-bias education for young children and ourselves*. National Association for the Education of Young Children.

Duncan-Andrade, J. M., & Morrell, E. (2008). *The art of critical pedagogy: Possibilities for moving from theory to practice in urban schools* (New ed.). Peter Lang Publishing.

Freeman, M., & Vasconcelos, E. F. S. (2010). Critical social theory: Core tenets, inherent issues. *New Directions for Evaluation, 2010*(127), 7–19. https://doi.org/10.1002/ev.335

Gause, C. (2008). From social justice to collaborative activism: Changing the landscape of academic leadership. *Academic Leadership: The Online Journal, 6*(3), Article 9. https://scholars.fhsu.edu/alj/vol6/iss3/9

Gay, G. (2002). Preparing for culturally responsive teaching. *Journal of Teacher Education, 53*(2), 106–116. https://doi.org/10.1177/0022487102053002003

Gillborn, D. (2009). Education policy as an act of White supremacy: Whiteness, critical race theory and education reform. *Journal of Education Policy, 20*(4), 485–505. https://doi.org/10.1080/02680930500132346

Kincheloe, J. L. (2003). *Teachers as researchers: Qualitative inquiry as a path to empowerment* (2nd ed.). RoutledgeFalmer.

Kliebard, H. M. (1989). Problems of definition in curriculum. *Journal of Curriculum and Supervision, 5*, 1–5.

Ladson-Billings, G. (1995). But that's just good teaching! The case for culturally relevant pedagogy. *Theory into Practice, 34*(3), 159–165. https://doi.org/10.1080/00405849509543675

Leonardo, Z. (2004). The color of supremacy: Beyond the discourse of "white privilege." *Educational Philosophy and Theory, 36*(2), 137–152. https://doi.org/10.1111/j.1469-5812.2004.00057.x

Loughran, J. (2002). Effective reflective practice: In search of meaning in learning and Teaching. *Journal of Teacher Education, 53*(1), 33–43.

Matsuda, M., Lawrence, C., Delgado, R., & Crenshaw, K. (Eds.). (1993). *Words that wound: Critical race theory, assaultive speech, and the First Amendment*. Westview Press.

National Center for Education Statistics. (2021). Characteristics of public-school teachers. https://nces.ed.gov/programs/coe/pdf/2021/clr_508c.pdf

Nieto, S. (2010). *The light in their eyes: Creating multicultural learning communities* (10th anniversary ed.). Teachers College Press.

Sawchuk, S. (2021). What is critical race theory, and why is it under attack? *Education Week*. https://www.edweek.org/leadership/what-is-critical-race-theory-and-why-is-it-under-attack/2021/05

Shannon, P. (1987). Special issue: The basal reader in American reading instruction. *The Elementary School Journal, 87*(3), 307–329. https://doi.org/10.1086/461502

Sleeter, C. E. (2008). Preparing White teachers for diverse students. In M. Cochran-Smith, S. Feiman-Nemser, D. J. McIntyre, & K. E. Demers (Eds.), *Handbook of research on teacher education* (3rd ed., pp. 559–582). Routledge.

Solorzano, D. G., & Bernal, D. D. (2001). Examining transformational resistance through a critical race and LatCrit theory framework: Chicana and Chicano students in an urban context. *Urban Education, 36*(3), 308–342.

Solorzano, D. G., & Yosso, T. J. (2020). Maintaining social justice hopes within academic realities: A Freirean approach to critical race/LatCrit pedagogy. *Denver Law Review, 7*(4), 595–621.

Steinberg, S. R., & Kincheloe, J. L. (2010). Power, emancipation, and complexity: Employing critical theory. *Power and Education, 2*(2), 140–151.

U.S. Department of Education. (2017). *Our nation's English learners: What are their characteristics?* https://www2.ed.gov/datastory/el-characteristics/index.html

Villa, E. (2010). *Interrupting the formation of teacher identities: Using inquiry to shift from teacher-centered to learner-centered* (Published Doctoral Dissertation). New Mexico State University.

Vought, R. (2020, September). Training in the Federal Government (M-20-34). Executive Office of the President. https://www.Whitehouse.gov/wp-content/uploads/2020/09/M-20-34.pdf?fbclid=IwAR1r7Ej2V0gZ8pNhIEjLtHDDNlfeYvBkzEgUfbrU3cXfot7RP2XKPwnCDe4

Wertsch, J. V. (1998). *Mind as action.* Oxford University Press.

Yosso, T. J. (2005). Whose culture has capital? A critical race theory discussion of community cultural wealth. *Race Ethnicity and Education, 8*(1), 69–91. http://dx.doi.org/10.1080/1361332052000341006

Zamudio, M., Russell, C., Rios, M. A., & Bridgeman, J. L. (2011). *Critical race theory matters: Education and ideology.* Routledge.

Chapter 6

Cross-Pollinating Teacher Preparation

Antiracist Inclusive Lesson Planning in Writers' Workshop

Amy Tondreau, Laurie Rabinowitz,
and Zachary T. Barnes

Too often, preservice teachers (PSTs) take a diversity course or an inclusion course that stands apart from methods courses, where they learn about antiracism and inclusion. However, they do not always learn the specific practices that align with these theories or have opportunities to connect those practices to curricular planning assignments. Yet, they are expected to integrate methods for supporting all students, including those with disabilities and those from marginalized backgrounds, once they have their own classrooms. This chapter presents a joint assessment to bridge antiracist, inclusive teaching across two methods courses as an approach for PSTs to learn about asset pedagogies and apply that knowledge to literacy lesson planning. Drawing on scholarship in Disability Critical Race Theory (DisCrit), Culturally Sustaining Pedagogy (CSP), and Universal Design for Learning (UDL) to design the assessment, students incorporate and annotate differentiation, co-teaching, and antiracist literacy practices in a lesson plan for writers' workshop.

Too often, PSTs take a diversity course or an inclusion course that stands apart from methods courses. In these diversity or inclusion courses, students learn about antiracism and inclusion. However, the content is often taught superficially and students do not always learn the specific practices that align with these theories or have opportunities to connect those practices to curricular planning assignments. Yet, they are expected to integrate methods for supporting all students once they have their own classrooms, including learners with disabilities and from marginalized backgrounds.

I (Amy) teach a writing methods class at a public university in the Southeastern United States where I aim to infuse antiracist teaching practices throughout the course, in addition to teaching writing content (e.g., craft moves and writing process) and practical methods for writing instruction (e.g., minilessons and strategy groups). In the summer of 2020, I began to reflect on the necessity of supporting PSTs in developing a sense of their own intersectional identities and those of their students to foster responsive, antiracist lesson planning and teaching practices. Balancing all these goals for the course proves challenging, as much of the content is quite new for my students. As I grappled with how to incorporate it all into one semester, I also sought a way to assess students' abilities to apply and integrate their new learning.

Bridging antiracist teaching across multiple courses seemed like a natural approach to provide PSTs with more space to explore their own identities and learn about asset pedagogies. It could also provide more time during my course to explore writing content and methods while still maintaining my philosophical commitment to antiracist teaching. An additional benefit of pairing courses was the opportunity to disrupt the silos of individual courses, which prevents PSTs from transferring much of their learning from one course to another. For example, PSTs were being taught co-teaching models (Friend, 2015) and UDL (Center for Applied Special Technology [CAST], 2018) in their Inclusion Methods course (taught by Zack) but were not applying those concepts to their literacy instruction planning in my course. Upon reflection, Zack and I realized that we were teaching our students about collaboration without modeling it for them.

Our problem of practice mirrors the literature, which indicates that disability identity is often absent from antiracist teaching (Annamma et al., 2016). While scholarship has begun to investigate how "race has figured prominently in special education" (Annamma et al., 2016, p. 12), it remains an under-explored topic in literacy teaching methods courses (Rabinowitz & Tondreau, 2021). Partnering with Zack in aligning our inclusion and writing methods courses, which students are expected to take in the same semester, seemed like a responsible and necessary next step in enhancing my antiracist teaching practice.

With this issue in mind, we share a joint summative assessment for a writing methods course and an inclusion course that we designed and iterated during the 2020–2021 academic year. In this assignment, students are asked to write a co-taught writing workshop lesson in response to specific classroom and focal learner profiles. To be more explicit about designing antiracist literacy instruction, students annotate these lessons to identify the instructional choices that demonstrate co-teaching models; UDL; and culturally sustaining, antiracist pedagogy.

TEACHING WITH A DISCRIT ORIENTATION

This assessment draws on scholarship in DisCrit, CSP, and UDL. DisCrit is a theoretical framework that explores how "both race and ability are socially constructed and interdependent" (Annamma et al., 2016, p. 13). The tenets of DisCrit align with antiracist teaching practices. More specifically, DisCrit focuses on troubling singular notions of identity, centering the voices of marginalized groups, and acknowledging Whiteness and Ability as property. In addition, DisCrit emphasizes the need to disrupt notions of normalcy that often circulate invisibly in seemingly neutral practices.

Historically, segregation and unequal treatment of individuals based on race have been justified through scientific racism (Annamma et al., 2016). While attitudes about intellectual inferiority of individuals based on their race have become less widespread, the legacy of this thinking remains rooted in the American school system. The overrepresentation of students from non-dominant racial and ethnic backgrounds in special education suggests that linkages between race and intellect may be undergirding our systems for disability identification (Harry & Klinger, 2014). DisCrit supports the unpacking of the normalized processes of racism and ableism so that educators may see how they are mutually reinforcing.

The Cross-Pollination of CSP and UDL

DisCrit provides a framework for exploring the experiences of students with disabilities and how to understand the school-based systems that reinforce racism and ableism. However, it is primarily a theoretical framework; consequently, it does not fully support educators in envisioning new teaching practices that may provide a more humanizing approach to teaching students of all identities, especially students with disabilities and students of color. To identify teaching practices that support a DisCrit orientation, we draw on a body of work that calls for the 'cross-pollination,' or exchange of ideas, between CSP and UDL (Waitoller & Thorius, 2016).

Building on previous scholarship in culturally relevant and responsive pedagogies (Ladson-Billings, 2014), CSP is an asset-based pedagogy that seeks to "sustain—linguistic, literate, and cultural pluralism as part of the democratic project of schooling" (Paris, 2012, p. 93). Educators who implement CSP commit to valuing multiple perspectives, affirming cultural competence, and developing critical consciousness. They also work to move beyond a heroes and holidays approach to curriculum that can essentialize students' cultures, races, and other identity categories (Banks, 2009). CSP works to incorporate intersectionality by valuing multiple identities into its framing; however, it has been lovingly critiqued for not explicitly attending to disability identities (Waitoller & Thorius, 2016).

UDL, another asset-based approach to teaching, is an instructional framework designed to foreground learner variability. Based on neuroscience research, the UDL framework does not name explicit teaching practices; instead, it provides a framework for educators to make instruction accessible. UDL has three organizing principles for designing curriculum: (a) provide multiple means of *engagement* to activate the 'why' of learning (i.e., the affective network), (b) provide multiple means of *representation* to activate the 'what' of learning (i.e., the recognition network), and (c) provide multiple means of *action and expression* to activate the 'how' of learning (i.e., the strategic network). While originally intended to support students with disabilities by making instruction and learning environments accessible, UDL has come to be understood as a tool for supporting students with a variety of ability levels due to its emphasis on designing instruction that is both accessible and challenging (Nelson, 2013). It also makes a strong companion for Friend's (2015) co-teaching models, which outline the different ways that educators might structure their classroom environment (see table 6.1). Integrating both UDL and co-teaching models provides educators with options for intentionally utilizing multiple adults in a classroom in purposeful ways.

Both CSP and UDL attend to the relationship between power and identity categories, call for critical curriculum consciousness that purposefully addresses the needs of a variety of learners from the outset, and establish a pedagogy where teachers learn from, not just about, marginalized students (Alim et al., 2017; Ladson-Billings, 2014; Rapp, 2015). Cross-pollinating these two methods for framing teaching practices allows practitioners to

Table 6.1 Co-teaching Models

Model	Description
Parallel Teaching	A class is split in half and one teacher teaches each half of the class
Station Teaching	Each teacher teaches a specific piece of content and the students rotate between these groups and independent groups
Alternative Teaching	One teacher teaches one small group while the other teacher works with the rest of the class. The small group could be working on something based on need, previewing upcoming content, or doing an extension activity
Team Teaching	Both teachers directly teach the class at the same time
One Teach, One Observe	One teacher leads the class while the other observes. The observing teacher might be paying attention to a particular student or collecting data on whole class understanding
One Teach, One Assist	One teacher leads the class while the other teacher provides targeted individual support

focus their teaching on "intersecting forms of oppression" (Alim et al., 2017, p. 4). Given that the overlaps of these orientations allow us to simultaneously attend to race and disability identity in curriculum and teaching practices, we chose to use a cross-pollinated CSP/UDL approach to designing our joint summative assessment.

Writers' Workshop

Exploration of the cross-pollination of CSP and UDL in literacy instruction has begun to develop in recent years (e.g., Coppola et al., 2019). However, this is a burgeoning field of research ripe for more robust study. While there has been some work exploring the intersection of CSP, UDL, and reading (e.g., Rabinowitz & Tondreau, 2021), there is a critical need to connect UDL, CSP, and writing. Writing instruction has been neglected, both in teacher preparation courses and in professional development. Falling under the umbrella of literacy instruction, writing is often tucked into courses, professional development, or curricular materials that focus heavily on reading (College Board, 2003; Dutro, 2010; Norman & Spencer, 2005). One of our aims is for PSTs to be well prepared as teachers of both reading and writing. Furthermore, given its already student-centered and flexible nature, the writers' workshop approach is well suited for CSP/UDL cross-pollination.

The writers' workshop is a pedagogical framework that aims to teach transferrable skills and strategies as children engage in the writing process that professional authors are thought to follow (Calkins, 1994). Educators who use this approach emphasize the meaning-making process of composition over mechanics and structure, along with the idea that children learn how to write through writing. In addition, the process model is committed to student engagement, emphasizing student agency through topic selection and authorship.

Graves (1985) noted that the writers' workshop is specifically supportive for students with language and literacy-based learning disabilities. It deemphasizes areas where many students with disabilities may struggle, such as "handwriting, spelling and language conventions," and instead "emphasizes what children know," writers' workshop provides students with disabilities increased access to writing and positive writing identities (Graves, 1985, p. 36). Those students can learn conventions over time as a tool to help them share meaning. Classroom practices such as small group instruction, one-to-one conferring, and student choice are well suited for CSP/UDL infusion and are already embedded in a writers' workshop approach. Our joint summative assessment served as a way for novice teachers to surface and build on elements of the writers' workshop that align with asset-based teaching approaches.

ANTIRACIST TEACHER EDUCATION PRACTICES AND IMPLEMENTATION: DESIGNING AND ITERATING A JOINT SUMMATIVE ASSESSMENT

The antiracist teacher education practices that follow are part of a design-based (Reinking & Bradley, 2008) study that explores how undergraduate teacher education students integrate CSP and UDL concepts into lesson planning for writers' workshops. Three iterations of the annotation assignment were completed across two different colleges of education in two different geographic regions of the United States. In this chapter, we reflect on the pilot, which was conducted in the northeast, and we draw on student work samples that were collected over two semesters at a university in the south. Following, we outline each version of the joint assessment, highlighting what we learned from each iteration. We believe this is a promising practice that may serve as an example that other teacher educators could implement in their own contexts. We believe that other institutions may be able to learn not only from the joint assessment that we share but also from our critical reflection on it and how we have worked to and continue to work to bend it toward the needs of our students.

An Incidental Pilot

The first iteration of this assignment came out of necessity in the summer of 2020. I (Laurie) was teaching a graduate course on disability to novice educators in a special education/general education dual master's degree program in a northeastern U.S. city. Given the challenges of the global pandemic and the protests for racial justice surrounding the murder of George Floyd, my students needed a reduced workload without undermining the integrity of their learning. I recognized that most of my students were cross enrolled in an education foundations course that focused on antiracist pedagogy. I reached out to the other faculty member to brainstorm a plan. Realizing that both courses included a curriculum writing project, the other faculty member and I crafted a joint co-taught antiracist accessible lesson planning project.

In my course, novice teachers were asked to attend to differentiation and co-teaching models in the design of their lesson plan, and in the other course, they were asked to attend to antiracist teaching practices. Rather than having them brainstorm generic differentiation ideas which were not student centered, I provided a focal learner or student profile (see Example of a Focal Student). Novice teachers were asked to plan a lesson in a three-column template, which had them highlight student actions, teacher actions, and points of accessibility (see table 6.2). To support the novice teachers in developing their lesson planning skills, I conferred with them about a draft of their lesson

Table 6.2   Three-Column Lesson Plan Template

Grade Level:
Standard(s):
Objective(s)
Materials and Resources:

Teacher Actions	Student Actions	Annotation
Lesson Launch/Connection		
Minilesson		
Independent Work Time/Small Groups/Conferences		
Link/Closure		

plans. They submitted the same lesson for both courses, but reflected on their lesson plans in my course with a focus on UDL and co-teaching as tools for accessibility and annotated the lesson plans for the other course with a focus on antiracist teaching. In doing this pilot joint co-taught project, I found that novice teachers benefited from additional context about the focal learners, and ultimately needed more than one focal learner to plan for. I had originally provided a focal learner who was hypothetically in the third grade, but several PSTs wanted to plan for primary grade students, so having multiple grades as options made a logical next step.

While reflecting on this project, I reached out to Amy, a critical friend and colleague, who teaches at another institution. She shared her problem of practice around finding the time to thoroughly integrate antiracist teaching into her writing methods course. After our conversation, we began brainstorming what it would look like to transfer this assignment into her context. At this point, Amy brought the idea of a shared assignment to Zack, a colleague at her university, as an opportunity to collaborate and support students in transferring and applying their learning across both the writing and inclusion courses.

Version 2.0: Crafting the Joint Assessment

For Amy and Zack to implement a joint assessment, we worked to philosophically align the content of our courses, ensuring that we both attended to ideas of CSP, antiracism, and inclusion. We also worked to ensure that the new assignment was geared toward undergraduate PSTs who had limited previous fieldwork experience. Not only were they entering with limited previous fieldwork experience, due to the ongoing pandemic during the 2020–2021 school year, PSTs were not able to participate in the typical 10–20 hr fieldwork placement that is typically a part of both courses. This meant that it was even more necessary—and challenging—to support PSTs in developing their skills in planning responsive instruction tailored with the needs of specific students in mind.

First, we had to shift the focus of the assignment from reading to writing; so, we revised the description of the focal classes and students to include information about individual writing skills and identities. We created two different classroom scenarios for the PSTs to choose from that included student demographics, typical structures for writing instruction, the genre of the unit, and the stage of the writing process. Setting one scenario in first grade and the other in fourth allowed PSTs to choose a preferred grade band. We also increased the number of focal student profiles to two for each scenario. Using composites of our collective teaching experience, we crafted descriptions of the students which included writing skills, interests, hobbies, families, ethnicities, linguistic backgrounds, disability classifications, and support services (see an example of a focal student below). We attended to details such as switching the sports teams the student supported to match our local context. More importantly, each student profile was asset focused and holistic, giving a fuller picture of who these students were as individuals in the classroom and in their communities. For example, Izzy's talent as an artist and storyteller shown below as a focal student is forefronted before we share that she is at the Letter/Word Representation stage of the writing process.

In this way, Izzy's literacy skills may be viewed through an asset lens. By including learner profiles that include all of these different characteristics of each individual student, we are encouraging PSTs to attend to ways to make instruction accessible and high interest, as well as culturally responsive.

Example of Focal Student

Izzy is a six-year-old Hispanic female. She attends first grade at an elementary school; this is her second year there. She is currently enrolled in an Integrated Co-Teaching Classroom for all subject areas and sees a Special Education Teacher in the resource room for pullout services 10 times a week (five periods of reading and five periods of Math for 30 min each), and five periods of push-in support (during writing). Izzy also receives related services from the Speech and Language Pathologists in a small group of three students, two times a week for 30 min.

In terms of her reading comprehension, Izzy loves read alouds during her small group work with the Special Education teacher and is able to retell some key moments from a read aloud with prompting and visuals. She also demonstrates a good relationship with her peers in her pullout group and is able to handle setbacks well. In whole class instruction, she often has difficulty maintaining her concentration during the whole class read alouds and needs prompts to stay focused. She has difficulty turning and talking with a partner in that setting and benefits from a teacher providing verbal sentence starters to help her respond to questions. She has been able to learn roughly two new sight-words a week and can confidently read: are, but, so, see, just, too, last, just, see, and now from the first 15 words of the Fry Sight Word List. She is able to name all the letters of the alphabet from visual memory when displayed both in lower and upper case. She is able to identify the sounds of 15 letters of the alphabet and often confused the short *e* and *i* sounds.

Izzy is a talented artist and can draw detailed pictures that include accurate representations of her environment. She is also able to verbally share stories about the images that she draws, elaborating on who is present in the images, what they are doing, and how they are behaving. Her writing indicates that she is in the Letter/Word Representation section of the Transitional stage of writing and the middle Letter Name Alphabetic spelling stage; she uses the first letter sound of each word to represent an entire word and can use letter–sound relationships. Izzy lives with her mother and younger brother. Her mother reports that Izzy is a kind older sibling and gets along well with her cousins. At home, it can take Izzy quite a bit of time to get ready in the morning and she often needs prompts to get dressed. Her mother reports that she would love ideas for helping Izzy to follow a series of steps with fewer

Table 6.3 Version 2.0 Lesson Plan Scoring Criteria

	Literacy Criteria	Inclusion Criteria	Total points
Mechanics of a lesson plan must include	Standard(s) & objective(s) Materials needed and resources used Lesson launch (hook or connection) Minilesson: skill & strategy Student independent work Small group/conferences Share/Closure		___/ 20
Application of literacy and antiracist pedagogy	Use of the concepts of Antiracist, Antibias teaching—how will you make sure your lesson is inclusive of all students' identities? How will this impact the modeling and resources you select? How will you evaluate it? Principles practices of writing instruction An assessment—how will you know your students have processed the lesson? What will they produce? How will you evaluate it? Annotate aspects of the plan that represent antiracist and progressive theory/practice and those which may be based on a different approach ("This is antiracist because . . .") Connect your choices to specific course readings		___/ 30
Application of inclusive pedagogy		Use of the concepts of UDL Use at least two instances of co-teaching and describe the specific type for each instance Two specific examples of planned supports for focus learners that show evidence of UDL	___/ 30
		Literacy Grade	___/ 50
		Inclusion Grade	___/ 50

prompts so that she can get Izzy to school on time. Currently, Izzy is missing the first half of the first period two times a week and this may potentially be impacting her access to instruction.

The use of focal profiles also allowed us to intentionally align this assignment with preparation for the edTPA, a high-stakes teaching performance assessment they must complete to apply for teacher certification. The edTPA requires teacher candidates to address how their lesson plans are responsive to both their class and to specific focal learners. As a part of the assignment, we expected PSTs to use their annotations to highlight how they were planning for multiple aspects of the focal learner profiles. For instance, PSTs were encouraged to not only view Izzy as a student who needed literacy remediation due to her speech and language classification, but also to lesson plan in a way that centered her storytelling skills and artistic abilities. As seen in the scoring tool's inclusion criteria (see table 6.3), PSTs were evaluated on their ability to name two specific examples of planned supports for focus learners and to show evidence of UDL. Furthermore, students are encouraged to think about Izzy's identities as a multilingual learner, and use the tenets of CSP to see her multilingualism as a strength that can be proactively incorporated into a lesson plan.

Amy and Zack introduced the assignment to PSTs collaboratively, explicitly sharing the origins and intent of the assignment with them. We highlighted how we were intentionally modeling co-teaching and collaboration and how our planning was responsive to the context of the pandemic and our prior experiences teaching this content. In doing this, we modeled for students how antiracist, inclusive educators are reflective and responsive practitioners. Another way we modeled collaborative teaching was by assigning some of the same readings. PSTs had the opportunity to build connections about CSP and UDL across courses in class discussions and assignments leading up to the shared summative assessment. PSTs were paired up to complete the assignment to have the experience of planning with a co-teacher. Zack went over the challenges of co-teaching and explained that this assignment mirrored the co-planning that occurs frequently in grade-level or departmentalized teacher teams in schools.

These instructional moves led to PSTs demonstrating an emergent ability to plan for the roles of multiple adults in a single lesson. In analyzing PSTs' lesson plans, we found that several partnerships were able to purposefully utilize two teachers to address the learning needs of the focal learners. Table 6.4 presents an example teaching partnership who used small groups to specifically support Izzy. With Izzy in mind, these PSTs planned a lesson launch focused on high frequency words. They also planned to embrace her linguistic identity by offering the opportunity to spell these words both in English and Spanish. This instruction connects her preexisting knowledge of the

Table 6.4 Small Group Targeted Differentiation

Teacher Actions	Student Actions	Annotation
Lesson Launch 6. Ms. A will be working with Manuel on vocabulary comprehension at Table One and Ms. X will be working with Izzy on sight-words at Table Two. Both will be with a small group of 4–6 students. 7. At the end of each 10 minute increment, both teachers will clap rhythmically one, two . . . three, four, five times. **Table One**. 8. Ms. A will begin by saying, "Friends, today we will be reviewing some of the vocabulary from the mentor text so that we can have a better understanding of the text." She will then give each student five pictures. A picture of an orchard, a dairy, grains, a mill, and wheat. 9. Ms. A will then place five sentence strips on the table. The sentence strips will have the words and kid-friendly definitions written on them. Ms. A will then hold up a sentence strip with the words facing the students, she will then read the strip.	7. The students will then stop what they are doing and respond with the same cadence. 8. The students will be instructed to echo Ms. A as she points to each word. 9. The students will be instructed to look through their pictures after hearing the word and definition and then hold up the picture that matches.	6. This demonstrates station teaching. Both teachers are working on the same subject, but providing more direct teaching that is specific to the needs of the students in that group. 7. This is to gain the students' attention. This provides a loud sound and a visual signal that will alert the student with a hearing impairment that it is time to transition to the next station. 8. This is to inform the students about the purpose of the lesson and to activate their prior knowledge. 9. This provides the students with the opportunity to practice fluency and helps strengthen the students' knowledge of print concepts and English vocabulary. This is supportive of the UDL framework because it offers a means of representation of language and symbols.

Note. This is an excerpt from PSTs' lesson plan; numbering indicates the correspondence between teacher actions, student actions, and annotations.

meaning of a word in Spanish with the English meaning and spelling; it also validates her identity as a Spanish speaker in an English-dominant classroom.

The lesson plan excerpt presented in table 6.4 demonstrates that the PST partnership understood how co-teaching could be used to provide culturally relevant and data-informed literacy instruction. However, these PSTs were still demonstrating emergent knowledge, since they inaccurately labeled the co-teaching terminology. They labeled their small group work as "station teaching," missing an essential component of the model: allowing students to rotate between groups. After reflecting, we agreed that they developed the more complex skill of using UDL and CSP to design accessible instruction but are still developing their academic pedagogical vocabulary to fully explain their instructional decision-making.

Amy and Zack also "strongly suggested" that PSTs submit a draft of their lesson plans and confer with us before submitting a final version. We found that pairs who attended these conferences submitted final versions of lesson plans that more closely aligned with the philosophical orientations outlined in assignment directions. One major benefit of the conferences was that they allowed us to interrupt misconceptions about inclusive pedagogy that were manifesting as students put their learning about co-teaching and student grouping into practice. Specifically, we found that students were replicating preexisting ideas about student grouping in their lesson planning rather than using data-informed decision-making. The tendency to group any students who need extra support in literacy together demonstrates how difficult it is to resist deeply rooted institutional discourses about disability, "struggling" readers and writers, and segregation, even when taking a course on inclusion (Spratt & Florian, 2015).

For instance, in one lesson plan, the PSTs wrote that during independent work time, one teacher would "work with Manuel, Izzy, and other students that need extra help in small groups to write an informative paragraph," explaining that students would "work on their own informative paragraph with the assistance of the co-ed teacher, to help them build more on what they are struggling with in writing." Here, the PSTs seem to assume that Manuel and Izzy's needs are the same simply because they are both identified as needing support, or perhaps because they were both identified as bilingual. After feedback during a conference, they revised their plan so that teachers would work with students, "in two groups: Manuel and four other students (group A) elaborating their writing. Izzy and three other students (group B) working on writing sentences based on their pictures." By meeting Manuel and Izzy's individual needs differently in the revised plan, this partnership exhibited a stronger understanding of inclusion by recognizing students' individual identities.

Version 3.0: Refining and Adjusting

Zack and Amy made several minor adjustments to the shared assignment for the following semester. These changes were driven by PST feedback and student work in an attempt to clarify aspects of the assignment that were confusing. Specifically, we aimed to be more explicit about our expectations, requesting that PSTs identify a co-teaching model for each section of the lesson plan and that they were welcome to use first person as they reflected on and annotated their lessons. We also clarified that the "Independent Work" section of the plan needed to indicate specific strategies that would be taught in either small groups or conferences. The sections of the lesson plan were divided up with new, more specific headings, to indicate the Connection/Lesson Launch, Teaching/Modeling, Active Engagement, and Share sections

Table 6.5 Adapted Lesson Plan Template

Grade Level:
Standard(s):
Objective(s)
Materials & Resources:

TEACHER ACTIONS	STUDENT ACTIONS	ANNOTATION
Lesson Launch/Connection (5 min)		
Teach, Active Engagement, Link of Minilesson (10 min)		
Independent Work Time/Small Groups/Conferences (30 min)		
Share Session to Close Workshop (5–10 min)		

of the writers' workshop, rather than the more general titles used previously. Suggested time frames were also added to each of these sections to help students pace out their lessons (see table 6.5 for the adapted lesson plan template). We also chose to bold and underline some of the most important information in each classroom scenario, such as the genre students were writing in and the stage of the process they were in, as these were commonly overlooked by PSTs when creating their lesson plans.

These minor adjustments provided PSTs with more explicit guidance about how to approach the assignment, and their lesson plans reflected more elaboration on how elements of the writers' workshop could be infused with UDL and CSP. For example, table 6.6 presents a partnership that effectively planned the role of both teachers throughout each section of their plan. Alongside their consideration of co-teaching structures, PSTs also made explicit references to UDL principles and the supports they implemented to provide access for students; they also explicitly identified the importance of racial representation when discussing the selected mentor text for the lesson. In this example, PSTs utilize a common practice of writers' workshop (studying the craft of a mentor text) and illustrate through their annotations the ways that this instructional choice is in alignment with the tenets of both UDL and CSP. They explain that their teaching "is UDL because it provides students with the tools needed to look back on the text rather than recall details," while their mentor text is "a culturally relevant text because it is about the students' hometown." The PSTs highlight that the racial identity of the main character is representative of the racial identity of the majority of the students, and the gender of the main character is particularly relevant to Janelle, one of the focal learners.

REFLECTION OF EFFECTIVENESS OF PRACTICE

Based on our description earlier, we believe that this is an effective antiracist inclusive joint assessment that other teacher educators could replicate and bend to their own contexts. Research suggests that co-taught higher education courses can benefit PSTs by providing examples of how they can effectuate co-teaching in their own classrooms and can also benefit teacher educators by supporting their cross-curricular content development (Bacharach & Heck, 2007; Lock et al., 2016). However, without college-wide support and funding for two instructors to lead one course, this model can be challenging to implement. We found that the partnering of two courses similarly offered PSTs examples of what co-teaching looks like in real time and they were able to see that the modeling of co-teaching practices transferred into lesson planning. Thus, the use of a joint assessment allowed for higher education co-teaching

Table 6.6 Lesson Planning for Co-teaching Example

Teacher Actions	Student Actions	Annotation
Minilesson **(Team teaching)** Teacher 1: The educator will read aloud *The Quickest Kid in Clarksville* by Pat Zietlow Miller. First, remind the students to pay attention to the way the author appeals to the five senses. Teacher 2: The educator will write and provide a drawing of the five senses on the board to remind the students what they are looking for. The students will be prompted to demonstrate what senses the author appealed to in the reading by touching either their mouth, nose, ears, hands, and eyes.	Students will break out into groups of three and be given one copy of the mentor text per group. Students will nonverbally respond using the directions.	Allows students to follow along while participating in a read aloud. This is UDL because it provides students with the tools needed to look back on the text rather than recall details. It also offers our student with a reading disability support as they may struggle independently. Students will be grouped according to their ZPD. This is a culturally relevant text because it is about the student's hometown. This is antiracist teaching because it recognizes and represents the identities of the majority of the students in the class. This text choice also engages Janelle because she enjoys texts that center on a female character. This is UDL because it gives students visual assistance and can be used for reference while finding examples. The use of this nonverbal response aids in the participation of students who would not normally contribute to the conversation. This total physical response is UDL because it provides alternate means of action and expression which caters to our student diagnosed with autism.

without requiring a system-wide restructuring of courses. Teacher educators might seek out opportunities where there is programmatic alignment between courses so that moments for co-teaching and co-assessment can be similarly capitalized on. Especially in institutions that use cohort models, partnering faculty to make connections about asset pedagogies across courses could prove beneficial.

Meeting with students for conferences proved to be essential in supporting PSTs with effectively completing this assignment. While the topics of antiracism, CSP, and inclusion had been taught throughout the semester, students did not have the opportunity to put these concepts into action due to the lack of classroom placements. Consequently, PSTs found annotating their lesson plans to explicitly name the antiracist and inclusive practices they included to be the most challenging element of the assignment. Several pairs of PSTs came to their meetings with little to nothing in the initial drafts of their annotation columns, and many expressed uncertainties about discussing how their pedagogical choices were or were not aligned with CSP and UDL.

Through our conversations during the meetings with students, we were able to engage PSTs in conversations about elements of writing workshop instruction that they had already included in their lesson plans but not highlighted in their annotations. Elements of workshop pedagogy are inherently antiracist and inclusive, but PSTs were not able to explicitly identify them as such. When we discussed these components of their plans, students were able to reflect on the ways that the elements of their pedagogy were responsive and built positive literacy identities for their students. They were able to see overlap in methodology between UDL moves and antiracist teaching moves, which helped them recognize that including more than one asset pedagogy in planning was less intimidating than they initially believed. While PSTs required scaffolding and prompting to do so, once they made these connections, most were able to create annotations that illustrated their understanding. Their increased understanding was also evident in many of their reflections on the process of completing the lesson planning assignment, where they were able to connect their choices to course readings and activities. We hope that these practices of annotating and cross-collaboration become replicable and habitual, so that antiracist and inclusive practices can be applied to all curricular planning.

MOVING FORWARD

Our reflections on this teaching practice suggest that intentionally planning with an antiracist framework can be challenging for novice educators. While they might be able to state an antiracist philosophical orientation, being able to intentionally choose teaching practices aligned with those beliefs and explain the rationale for those decisions requires significant practice. Being able to practice this type of theory-informed decision-making across paired courses, with the support and perspective of more than one faculty member, provided a foundation for developing these skills. However, while our assessment encouraged PSTs to consider the intersections of race and disability in the design of their lesson plans, other essential aspects of the focal students' identities, such as their gendered experiences, were left largely absent from the joint key assessment. Since we believe that antiracist teachers should forefront the multidimensional nature of individual student identity (Paris & Alim, 2014), other social identities should be incorporated into student annotations. Intersectional understandings of identity might be forefronted in foundational theory courses. This would allow for joint assessments in methods courses wherein students annotate across multiple identity lenses without having to learn about intersectional identities at the same time.

Another step forward in this work is to support novice educators in better understanding how asset-informed teaching practices can benefit students for multiple reasons or benefit multiple student profiles at the same time. To develop a deepened understanding of the overlapping benefits of various teaching practices across multiple asset pedagogies, novice educators need multiple opportunities to identify, name, and connect teaching practices across more than one framework. Teacher education programs might accomplish this by integrating multiple asset frameworks, as we did in our joint assessment, into all teaching methods courses. Integrating multiple asset frameworks would also support newer educators in recognizing that asset-based teaching practices are not solely tied to a particular framework, but rather may mutually benefit students across a variety of different identity factors.

REFERENCES

Alim, H. S., Baglieri, S., Ladson-Billings, G., Paris, D., Rose, D. H., & Valente, J. M. (2017). Responding to "cross-pollinating culturally sustaining pedagogy and universal design for learning: Toward an inclusive pedagogy that accounts for dis/ability." *Harvard Educational Review, 87*(1), 4–25. https://doi.org/10.17763/1943-5045-87.1.4

Annamma, S. A., Connor, D. J., & Ferri, B. A. (2016). Touchstone text: Dis/ability critical race studies (DisCrit): Theorizing at the intersections of race and Dis/ability. In D. J. Connor, B. A. Ferri, & S. A. Annamma (Eds.), *DisCrit: Disability studies and critical race theory in education* (pp. 9–32). Teachers College Press.

Bacharach, N., & Heck, T. W. (2007). Co-teaching in higher education. *Journal of College Teaching & Learning, 4*(10), 19–26. https://doi.org/10.19030/tlc.v4i10.1532

Banks, J. (2009). Multicultural education: Dimensions and paradigms. In J. Banks (Ed.), *International companion to multicultural education* (pp. 9–32). Routledge.

Calkins, L. M. (1994). *The art of teaching writing.* Heinemann.

CAST. (2018). *Universal design for learning guidelines,* version 2.2. http://udlguidelines.cast.org

College Board. (2003). *The neglected "R": The need for a writing revolution.* The National Commission on Writing in America's Schools.

Coppola, R., Woodward, R., & Vaughn, A. (2019). And the students shall lead us: Putting culturally sustaining pedagogy in conversation with universal design for learning in a middle-school spoken word poetry unit. *Literacy Research: Theory, Method, and Practice, 68*(1), 226–249. https://doi.org/10.1177/2381336919870219

Dutro, E. (2010). What 'hard times' means: Mandated curricula, class-privileged assumptions, and the lives of poor children. *Research in the Teaching of English, 44*(3), 255–291. https://doi.org/10.17763/1943-5045-86.3.366

Friend, M. M. (2015). Welcome to co-teaching 2.0. *Educational Leadership, 73*(4), 16–22.

Graves, D. (1985). All children can write. *Learning Disabilities Focus, 1*(1), 36–43.

Harry, B., & Klinger, J. (2014). *Why are so many minority students in special education: Understanding race and disability in schools*. Teachers College Press.

Ladson-Billings, G. (2014). Culturally relevant pedagogy 2.0: a.k.a. the remix. *Harvard Educational Review, 84*(1), 74–84. https://doi.org/10.17763/haer.84.1.p2rj131485484751

Lock, J., Clancy, T., Lisella, R., Rosenau, P., Ferreira, C., & Rainsbury, J. (2016). The lived experience of instructors co-teaching in higher education. *Brock Education Journal, 26*(1), 22–35. https://doi.org/10.17763/haer.84.1.p2rj131485484751

Nelson, L. L. (2013). *Design and deliver: Planning and teaching using universal design for learning*. Brooks Publishing.

Norman, K. A., & Spencer, B. H. (2005). Our lives as writers: Examining preservice teachers' experiences and beliefs about the nature of writing and writing instruction. *Teacher Education Quarterly, 32*(1), 25–40.

Paris, D. (2012). Culturally sustaining pedagogy: A needed change in stance, terminology, and practice. *Educational Researcher, 41*(3), 93–97. https://doi.org/10.17763/1943-5045-86.3.366

Paris, D., & Alim, H. S. (2014). What are we seeking to sustain through culturally sustaining pedagogy? A loving critique forward. *Harvard Educational Review, 84*(1), 85–100. https://doi.org/10.17763/1943-5045-86.3.366

Rabinowitz, L., & Tondreau, A. (2021). Balancing literacies: UDL/CSP-infused elementary reading instruction. In C. McCray (Ed.), *Multifaceted strategies for social emotional learning and whole learner education* (pp. 86–120). IGI Global.

Rapp, W. H. (2015). *Universal design for learning in action: 100 ways to teach all learners*. Brooks Publishing.

Reinking, D., & Bradley, B. A. (2008). *On formative and design experiments: Approaches to language and literacy research*. Teachers College Press.

Spratt, J., & Florian, L. (2015). Inclusive pedagogy: From learning to action. Supporting each individual in the context of 'everybody'. *Teaching and Teacher Education, 49*, 89–96. https://doi.org/10.1016/j.tate.2015.03.006

Waitoller, F. R., & Thorius, K. A. K. (2016). Cross-pollinating culturally sustaining pedagogy and universal design for learning: Toward an inclusive pedagogy that accounts for dis/ability. *Harvard Educational Review, 86*(3), 366–389. https://doi.org/10.17763/1943-5045-86.3.366

Chapter 7

A Curriculum of Accomplicity

Foundations, Concepts, and Actions for Justice Work in Education

Morna McDermott McNulty

The author proposes a framework for mostly, but not exclusively, White educators to reject the comforts of calling themselves allies in the antiracist movement, arguing instead for educators to embrace the role of accomplice. The chapter identifies distinctions between being a White ally and a White accomplice, arguing that the former is insufficient for transforming systemic levels of oppression while the latter demands White discomfort and radical reimagining of the relationships between space/place, power, and privilege. The chapter provides a framework of foundations, concepts, and actions necessary for developing a praxis of accomplicity. This praxis reconceptualizes modes of inquiry that create a curriculum of contradictions and complexities. This chapter suggests that a curriculum for accomplicity conceptualizes a foundation of being/becoming that is collective, collaborative, and compassionate. It calls for actions to engage the accomplice in radical interchanges of self, 'Other,' and structural oppression.

> I have never been more aware of the difficulty of witness—that is, how awful it is to look, how awful it is to look away; how little I have to say and how important it is that I say it. The book is not about genocide, but genocide is a scar that runs the length of it, the horror I have no right to tell, yet no right to ignore.
>
> —Laura Apol, *Poetry, Poetic Inquiry and Rwanda*, 2021

INTRODUCTION

The aim of this chapter is to propose a framework for mostly, but not exclusively, White[1] educators (such as myself[2]) to reject the comforts of calling themselves *allies* in the antiracist movement, arguing instead for educators to embrace the role of *accomplice*. To accomplish this, the chapter explores the following questions: *How do teachers teach and students learn within the context of troubling knowledge?* And, *how can we teach and learn toward becoming accomplices to social justice, even when the recognition of being an accomplice means understanding one's complicity in systems of oppression* (Sheridan, 2017)? The answers to these questions challenge the consolidating of progressive (i.e., liberal) narratives into recycled paradigms that frame social justice coalitions and allies within 'acceptable' terms, that is, acceptable to the White society. In other words, the recycled ally paradigm oftentimes positions White educators in a Savior syndrome where they are depicted as "those who assist and People of Color as those who need assistance, thereby maintaining oppressive hierarchies" (Powell & Kelly, 2017, p. 42). This ideology can re-entrench itself as a liberatory narrative within hegemonic restrictors. Harden and Harden-Moore (2019) write:

> In terms of diversity, equity and inclusion, ally is an empty buzzword. It takes more than support to make a difference. White people claim to support the principles of diversity, equity, and inclusion; few, however, are courageous enough to put their own jobs on their line by speaking out against prejudice and discrimination in the workplace. (para. 6)

WHAT IS AN ACCOMPLICE?

According to Marcus (1997), accomplicity is a "state of being complex or involved" (p. 85). For the purposes of the argument in this chapter, I do not mean an accomplice as a person of complicity (Sheridan, 2017), nor one of White complicity (Applebaum, 2010). Rather, complicity used in the context here "highlights the individual's proximity to the problems . . . rather than separation from them" (Probyn-Rapsey, 2007, p. 69). For educators, this definition suggests proximity to students of color and their communities. Being an accomplice includes "teaching about the knowledge that we often resist learning" (Kumashiro, 2004, p. 10) because this includes "discomforting knowledge about our own complicity with oppression" (p. 17).

There are key distinctions between being an ally and being an accomplice. While an ally attends events where they can challenge White dominance and educate those present, the accomplice engages in three distinct practices that the ally does not: (a) they work from a fundamental belief that all freedoms and liberations are bound together; (b) they allow their actions to be informed/directed by leaders who are Black, Brown, First Nations/Indigenous, and/or People of Color (Osler, n.d.); and (c) they take actions that directly challenge institutionalized oppression with great personal risk to themselves. Allies seek ways of integrating People of Color into participation within existing power structures while maintaining the existing privileges their Whiteness affords them. By contrast, accomplices want to dismantle the existing power structures and redesign power relationships in order to decolonize[3] democracy and decenter the White narratives that shape educational practices.

So, what does a curriculum of accomplicity *look like*? How does one theorize transformation in the classroom and communities, in ways that are simultaneously systemic and personally internalized? This chapter explores the necessary traits and actions educators need to transition from ally to accomplice. To this end, a curriculum for accomplicity radically[4] conceptualizes a foundation of being/becoming that is collective (communal), collaborative (relational agency), and compassionate (affective). A curriculum of accomplicity theorizes a public praxis that calls for actions to engage the accomplice in radical interchanges of self, 'Other,' and structural oppression.

IMPLICATIONS FOR TEACHER EDUCATION RESEARCH AND PRACTICE

This chapter uses an organizing chart (figure 7.1) to explore and connect facets of theory and practice which together offer an approach for educators (or anyone) working as an accomplice. The foundation, concepts, and actions identified in this organizing chart (figure 7.1) each contain a series of

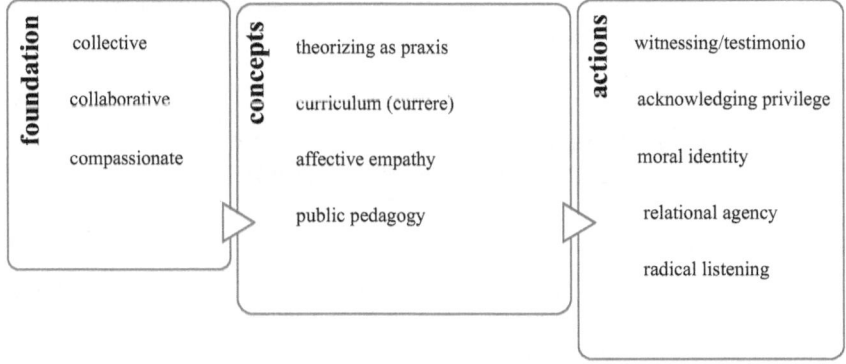

Figure 7.1 Foundations, Concepts, and Actions for Curriculum of Accomplicity.

qualitative experiences, or descriptions, which are necessary for developing an accomplicity framework.

Foundation of Values Embodied in a Curriculum of Accomplicity

A foundation is usually a cornerstone, or structure, that supports something. So, what is required to support accomplicity work? The accomplice must do more than just listen (Harden & Harden-Moore, 2019). The accomplice, an educator or otherwise, must stand with/beside those who are being attacked at the risk of their own physical, emotional, or professional safety or security. But what does this look like in the classroom? And how does one begin? The indispensable foundation of an accomplicity curriculum is built on 3 C's: collective (communal), collaborative (relational agency), and compassionate (affective). These values become the foundational structure of a theory that drives action.

A framework of accomplicity honors and upholds practices grounded in collective knowledge and wisdom that create *collective* power (Harjo, 2019). The accomplice embodies "mapped experiences of performance" (Daspit & McDermott, 1990, p. 51); these are moments and spaces where bearing witness may occur. In other words, "the performative enactment of witnessing creates 'effects of truth' and transforms the narrative of victim to that of an agent" (Chaturvedi, 2015, p. 2). It is also vital to find means by which *compassion* can replace ego. Compassion (and perhaps also empathy) is evoked via an affective dimension of the conscious awareness of the experience of others (Giroux, 2013). Consciousness is a "felt quality" (Chalmers, 2010, p. 20); to become conscious of one's biases and privilege is to "feel" (as a performance of body, mind, and spirit) an experience. A *collaborative* assemblage of these conscious experiences arranges (and in circular fashion is arranged by) the concept for a framework for action. These three "C" qualities permeate the concepts and actions of the framework.

DEFINING THE CONCEPTS FOR AN ACCOMPLICITY FRAMEWORK

Affective Theorizing

To theorize, as the term is being used in this chapter, means to develop a set of ideas (through affective remembering) that are organized in a fashion to influence the ways we are to be, to live, and the *how* and the *why* of our interconnected experiences. It is to make *sense* in ways that are not only intellectual, but literally *sense-ory* (i.e., relating to our affective ways of being). In this way, theoretical knowledge is healing; a change of self and the outer/world, or in the words of bell hooks (1991), "I saw in theory then a location for healing" (p. 4).

In addition, contrary to conventional scientific definitions, which define theory as an abstract and disconnected process from *doing*, I argue theorizing *is not* the opposite of practice; it is embedded *in* practice. Theorizing means to re-sense, or to feel an emergence of what *is*, simultaneously with what *could be* by way of "possible futures" (hooks, 1994, p. 61). To theorize is to witness *in and as the act of theorizing* social change. It is to elevate a complicated composite of aesthetic, epistemological, affective, psychological, political, spiritual, and social elements.

Curriculum

Curriculum, within the context of an accomplicity framework, does not imply a set of pedagogical steps or specific learning materials. It is not a lesson plan, nor a given subject area. Rather, I am borrowing from the curriculum of the Anthropocene which forms the "conceptual and sensory tools" (Anthropocene Curriculum, 2021, para. 3) necessary to run the "circuits of epistemic and aesthetic loops that inform the way earthly creatures can survive, thrive, and collaborate in a knot of conflicting concerns, needs, and ways of life" (para. 8). This definition echoes elements of *currere* (Pinar, 1978), which understands curriculum "as the course in a race" (Pinar, 1994, p. 13) in which one examines their past, present, and future selves. Pinar (1994) argues that *currere* is "the building of the self, the lived experience of subjectivity" (p. 220). The curriculum is the track of one's experiences, and *currere* is the lens through which one constructs meaning. Through *currere*, one can reflect, analyze, and deconstruct experiences to theorize alternative or multiple meanings of educational events.

As part of an accomplice curriculum, the educator engages in all four phases of the *currere* experience. In the first phase, *regressive*, an individual recalls the past. In the second, *progressive*, phase one pauses in the present to think about the future (bracketing it, as such), characterized by a reflection on the possibilities for the future in terms of how they manifest themselves in the present. The third, *analytical*, phase is when one analyzes the past and the future in light of the process of recalling the past. This may also be called recursion. As Pinar (1978) contends, the analytic stage asks us to answer the following question, "How is the future present in the past, the past in the future, and the present in both?" (p. 312). Finally, in the *synthetical* phase, an individual determines meaning and encourages imagined transformation.

As an accomplice, it is during the third phase of *currere*, in bracketing the past and future, that the accomplice can pause their own personal narrative, and stand alongside—like "with-ness as witness" (Apol, 2021, p. 21)—an alternative narrative, one which offers a different history that disrupts how we see ourselves in relationship to that history. *Currere* in this fashion takes us from the *I* to the *We* (T. Poetter, personal communication, June 4, 2019). This extensive process of self-reflection through *currere* becomes a way to shift the language used in the formation of identity and of our relationships—our obligation—to others, and to a transformation of structural inequities and the language we use to retell our history. Going a step further, the accomplice can explore critical feminist *currere* (Baszile, 2015), which is committed to a process of self-actualization toward well-being and self-actualization for the purpose of "decolonizing the mind" (p. 199).

To engage in such acts of critical self-actualization, the educator-as-accomplice transforms not only what they *know*, but what they *believe*. By participating in the four phases of *currere*, the educator is doing memory work; excavating, deconstructing, and analyzing how one comes to the beliefs and assumptions that they hold about themselves and others; and that will influence present and future actions in their practice.

Affective Empathy: Re/membering

As discussed previously, an affective approach to curriculum is concerned with the experience of beliefs, feelings, and attitudes. It is about understanding that people are not changed by facts as much as they are changed by moments that affect their sensory systems and worldviews. Through the process of *currere*, the educator can recall and re/member (rearrange one's memory) and actualize a different relationship to those events and persons. A curriculum of accomplicity parallels the work of Laura Apol (2021) whose poetic inquiry called for an affective relationality of "with-ness" (p. 3) and bearing "witness" (p. 3). An accomplice does not stand beside and watch/report, but is willing to be intertwined across, and through, every facet of being (or becoming) within a collective persistent positionality of action. It is to not only be an observer of a crisis but also be a participant who focuses on the social structures that are interwoven within our lived experiences (Apol, 2021). To participate in (re)membering one's history in light of shared present circumstances is to embody the effect of collective affective experiences in shaping our shared reality.

Affective modes of theorizing invite opportunities to bear witness to difficult knowledge (Britzman, 2000) as an "intersection of language, desire, power, bodies, social structure, materiality, and trauma" (Zembylas, 2014, p. 410). Difficult knowledge is generated through moments of witness because "the notion of atrocity is linked inextricably with witnessing" (Richardson, 2016, p. 674). It does not simply ask that I empathize with or become aware of the trauma of others. To witness as an accomplice means to renegotiate my own position of comfort, to focus on transferring the trauma of others into my struggle, the results of which benefit them rather than myself. It means to bear witness to the trauma of others and acknowledging the effect of my own Whiteness as being directly or indirectly complicit in these events. By contrast, a state of aversion is "the physiological impact of conflict and stress prompts the brain to release cortisol and adrenaline into the bloodstream, putting the body into a fight, flight, or freeze response" (Jackson, 2019, para 3).

Social aversion has been evident during the 2020–2021 debates about the inclusion (or perceived inclusion) of critical race theory (CRT) being taught in K–12 schools (Saunders, 2021). CRT has become the boogeyman for conservatives, causing a severe backlash by White people that is similar to Adorno's (1998, as cited in Britzman, 2014) description of "psychical pathologies of denial, projection, collective delusions (and) defenses against responsibility for mass murder" (p. 9). Oftentimes, White backlash to criticisms of the myth of American progress or American exceptionalism stems from the urge to disassociate from feelings of guilt and shame for one's personal or ancestral association with acts of terror or oppression, such as slavery. Accomplicity relies on affective, collective, and empathetic means for White people to get beyond aversion, or avoidance, of issues that invoke discomfort, and to become "capable of withstanding the demands of historical memory . . . in defense of those who are vulnerable" (Britzman, 2014, p. 6).

Public Pedagogy

The foundational qualities of collectivity, collaboration, and compassion work together to engage an accomplice critically in public pedagogical spaces: physically, intellectually, and emotionally. The concept of a public pedagogy decenters the importance of the academic venue or intellectual power reserved for the privileged, who are usually White and Eurocentric discursive spaces. As a pedagogy, it asks the questions: *Whose idea of 'public' is of importance?* And, *who is included or excluded in our definition of 'public'?* The concept of *public spaces* (including public schools) has been under attack ever since places and policies became racially integrated in the 1950s–1970s, and this attack was accelerated during the 1980s and Reagan's push toward privatization of public goods and services (see Strauss, 2018).

Within the framework of accomplicity theorizing, public pedagogy is also connected with the Black public sphere (Black Public Sphere Collective, 1995) as a critical social imaginary in "the world of magazines and coffee shops, salons and highbrow tracts" (p. 31). It marks a wider sphere of critical practice and visionary politics, in which "intellectuals can join with the energies of the street, the school, the church, and the city to constitute a challenge to the exclusionary violence of much public space in the United States" (p. 31). The accomplice acts as a witness to and participates under the leadership of the Black public sphere to foster resistance in wider publics and persuade outsiders to change their viewpoints on oppressive practices. At the same time, a White accomplice respects the sanctity of Black and Brown spaces, understanding when their presence may be more problematic than helpful.

Developing a Curriculum of Accomplicity in Action

What Does It Mean to "Bear Witness"?

While we often assume witnessing is simply an act of seeing, when we use the phrase to 'bear witness' it refers to experiencing the act of seeing and articulating something as a process of physical, emotional, or psychological weight. Witnessing means embracing a "theorization of difficult knowledge that has a political and activist orientation" (Zembylas, 2014, p. 391). Accomplicity demands an active witnessing that includes production of evidence, demonstration of a truth, implied proximity, and ethical demands made upon the listener. We must remember that the notion of 'bearing witness' is "woven deeply into the historic narratives about human rights violations against marginalized groups" (Richardson, 2016, p. 675).

How does the seeing, or the telling, become a tool of transformation? Witnessing is not merely seeing with the disembodied eye. Seeing, as such, decenters marginalized persons into the position of a specter, ghost, or apparition whose presence has little material effect. To witness is to be fully present *with* something, or someone; it requires being about something greater than yourself and a willingness to let go of control. The act of witnessing in this sense takes on a spiritual element, though not necessarily a religious one. It adheres to no theological doctrine, but concedes that witnessing, like other spiritual practices, "is about letting go and unlearning" (Rohr, 1989, p. 10).

To witness is a temporal and spatial experience demarcating a moment of one's being with-ness a conscious act of 'moment-ing' with intention toward etching the observation into action or deliberate purpose. It is this thread of turning toward, or with another which brings the inner into outer being, and collective external systems into transformational entanglements with the sticky layers of individual identity reconstruction. Yet, it is also a theory of contradictions. It is to hold a theory of both/and about oneself rather than either/or. We must hold the idea that I can change nothing but myself, while also decentering the *self* and knowing there is no *I* than that which is inextricably intertwined with the *we*. I am reminded of the myth of Coyote, the shape-shifting trickster who, according to Clifford et al. (2001), embodies the spirit of those cast as *Other* in our society. I concur with their observation that "what happens to him, happens to us" (p. 9). The accomplice knows that self-survival depends upon the survival of others, not at the expense of others.

Testimonio

The concept of testimonio, according to Lewis-Beck et al. (2004), is "generally defined as a first-person narration of socially significant experiences in which the narrative voice is that of a typical or extraordinary witness or protagonist" (p. 120) that disrupts dominant Eurocentric narratives. In the service to the concept of a public pedagogy, such testimonios relay the significance of a public event for a community or people, a change of, or on, systemic oppression. Testimonio becomes a radical counter narrative to the narrative of White aversion or mythical reappropriations of justice (Hunn et al., 2006). Testimonio is also an effective medium for affective curricula in that it often includes "sight, sense, smell, and sound" (Giroux, 2013, p. 83) as part of its narrative elements.

For White accomplices, listening to testimonio is the opportunity to radically reimagine their own stories, and to have a profound psychic change which, to have any effect, must be followed by action. Moving from ally to accomplice means challenging the consolidation of the progressive narrative into a recycling of old paradigms that frames social justice coalitions and allies within acceptable terms. More than mere storytelling, testimonios are deliberate and politically embedded acts of oral and written expression—understood as purposeful forms of resistance or "legacies of reflexive narratives of emancipation" (Pentón Herrera & Obregón, 2020, p. 384). Testimonio provides fertile opportunities in "reflexive spaces" (ibid, p. 385) for reexamining one's relationship to privilege and provokes active willingness to transform that system. These relationships with accomplices are "realized through mutual consent and build trust. They (the accomplice) don't just have our backs; they are at our side, or in their own spaces confronting and unsettling colonialism" (Indigenous Action Media, 2015, p. 86).

Starting with a theory of accomplicity, one includes a radical decentering of the ego while simultaneously worrying about changing no one but the self. But what does it mean, as a teacher with racial privilege, to carry the thread of messages across history of those who have suffered at the hands of White privilege? And how does an educator begin theorizing accomplicity as a mode of interrelational thinking, being, and becoming? A curriculum of accomplicity requires a praxis in which one (a) acknowledges and also decenters their own privilege, (b) develops a moral identity, (c) engages with a radical agency, and (d) supports radical listening.

Foregrounding One's Own Power and Privilege

Foregrounding privilege and power means that accomplicity is a multitiered geography and works beyond the direct and personal forms of oppression defined as merely "individual prejudice or pathology" (Tiger, 2015, p. 49). It includes "patriarchy, class war, antiblackness, and anti-immigrant racism" (p. 49). Toxic networks in teaching and educational policies reach into the seemingly more abstract systemic racism, the kind more elusive to many White educators. Often unconscious or subtle, these forms of racism implicate even the "progressively minded" educators among us. The history of public education and teacher education often ignores "structural consequences of national borders, capitalistic economies, state policies, and long histories of Black slavery, segregation, and colonialism" (p. 49).

Fully conceding the role of privilege means acknowledging that the teacher-as-accomplice has the opportunity to stay or leave the site of trauma (as a choice), unlike those who live it, and that the danger of speaking for another is to retraumatize through colonization-style narratives. Yet, the accomplice can neither dismiss nor avoid their moral complicity. Dawes (2007, as cited in Apol, 2021) summarizes this complexity of power and identity as "I do not have the right to speak. But at the same time, I do not have the right not to speak. I am stranded between the poles of entitlement and obligation" (p. 65). The accomplice does not evade this contradiction, but confronts it.

Moral Identity

By engaging in a process of *currere* (as described previously in the foundation for accomplicity), the accomplice can move away from self-interest and self as the locus of motive for decision-making and action. Teachers doing accomplice work can examine their own educational history and look for unconscious patterns and reexamine bias. Historically, most White progressives champion a social justice narrative so long as it does not affect their personal levels of comfort or access to privilege. There must be an acceptance on the teacher's part of their own moral entanglement within the system. The accomplice is "not emotionally fragile" (Osler, n.d., para. 3). The identity of an accomplice-teacher is tied to acceptance that within White supremacy exists an "attitude that individuals can voluntarily choose to relinquish" (Tiger, 2015, p. 50). The accomplice confronts the institutional arrangements in schooling curriculum, pedagogy, and policies.

In spaces of accomplicity within a group means remaining vigilant toward systems of power. Oppression and prejudice can re-present themselves within liberal or progressive spaces when left unchecked. Detangling from these systems requires a call to action to being inner active between the interior space of critical self-awareness and external sociopolitical movements. In other words, "What you're not changing, you are choosing" (Will, 2019, para. 10). The moral imperative of an accomplice in classroom interactions compels one "to become accountable and responsible to each other, that is the nature of trust" (Indigenous Action Media, 2014, para. 1).

Relational Agency

A curriculum of accomplicity acknowledges that the freedoms and liberations for all are inextricable and intertwined. To build agency by relationships, one must confront the face of oppressive structures. Through *currere*, while both upholding and rejecting one's position of privilege, the accomplice reexamines selfhood and subjectivity "as defined by co-existence, connectedness and compassion" (Apol, 2021, p. 208). In addition, relational agency requires resisting the language of co-optation, such as using the language of the community in a classroom to bring acts of resistance under the umbrella of civil, or modes of acceptable behavior as defined by privilege and power. The agency—actions or message—of oppressed persons or groups cannot be hijacked or co-opted by Whiteness in the effort of accomplices to support antiracist movements.

To be an accomplice means finding how to engage empathetically without co-opting the *experience* of another. This is particularly true in a classroom environment. The accomplice follows the lead of communities in struggle and remains ethically accountable to them (Tiger, 2015). For educators, being informed by the community of their classroom, they must find ways to connect with their students while avoiding speaking "for them" (Tiger, 2015, p. 56) or adopting a superficial form of relating. To develop radical empathy requires a form of listening that extends beyond the search for surface knowledge about their students.

Radical Listening

Radical listening is not leaning in (Sandberg, 2013); it is not waiting for the "powerful to renounce their privilege" (Tiger, 2015, p. 56) or looking for cultural inclusion. In keeping with the ideas of bearing witness, and specifically testimonio, it means hearing things the accomplice may not want to hear. Theorizing accomplicity pushes beyond a confessional mode of rejecting one's Whiteness as the end goal. Focus on the confession ironically places the attention back on the White person and away from the external actions which necessitate actual shifts in power. Empathy building and affective pedagogy do not suggest that through any witnessing or learning can Whiteness ever claim to now 'get,' or now 'know' what it is like to embody the marginalized lives of another.

In the case of radical listening, difficult knowledge (Britzman, 2000) invites deeply unsettling and evocative aversive responses. Sometimes this knowledge leaves the accomplice feeling implicated in those very systems that have caused trauma, leaving one to flail and stumble through a complicated terrain of guilt, fear, or confusion. Such classroom exchanges can invoke feelings of helplessness or nihilism (e.g., "why bother? I will never be able to change anything" or "no matter what I do, it's the wrong thing"). Furthermore, for many educators "imagining ways to disrupt such systems may seem overwhelming, impossible even" (Powell & Kelly, 2017, p. 43). The unconscious instinct of White accomplices might be to focus on getting it right, or to avoid making mistakes, feeling paralyzed by saying the wrong thing in response to witnessing trauma. The instincts of many teachers to avoid being implicated in racist systems, or fear of failure, are rooted in privilege, placing the feelings of oneself—or how one might be perceived—as being more important than the traumatic events or persons affected.

By contrast, for the accomplice, it means, as Farley (2009) points out, "having to tolerate the loss of certainty in the very effort to know" (p. 543). Instead of interpreting Black stories through a comfortable White Liberal Lens, White accomplices ought to allow stories of testimonio to serve as a vehicle for reinterpreting *themselves*, and how they use Whiteness as the patina upon which to paint history. The instinct of privilege might be to look for solutions that cater to liberal "white middle class consumption" (Tiger, 2015, p. 55).

Empathy must be more than a spectacle of observation. Empathy becomes more critical in that it "isn't just listening" (Milstein, 2015, p. 513) or responding with words of kindness or affection. Empathy for the accomplice is not an emotion, it is an action—an action which "brings difficulty into the light so it can be seen by all" (Milstein, 2015, p. 513) and means committing oneself to a set of behaviors that go above and beyond our individual inclinations which create solidarity through empathy. In the process of negating the "self" we are able to transform the self.

METHODS OF ACCOMPLICITY-AS-INQUIRY

Theorizing a framework of transformative action is closely interwoven with methods of inquiry. Inquiry is a process of theorizing through action by examining the self, the world, and how we construct meaning upon which we choose our future and map our theories. Ellsworth (2005) argues that a relational learning experience acknowledges that to be "alive and to inhabit a body is to be continuously and radically in relation with the world, with others, and with what we make of them" (p. 4). Bearing witness itself can be a method for researching oppression and resistance (Fine, 2006). As such, a question central to accomplicity-as-inquiry is, "How do researchers contribute to the interruption of the passive revolution?" (Fine, 2006, p. 86).

Narrative Inquiry

Bearing witness in the form of testimonio—as a narrative form of inquiry—relates educators to the world through a language that facts and statistics alone cannot. Storytelling, for example, might allow one to relate to another's experience that is not like their own and promotes empathy. Narrative inquiry assembles multiple points of voice and interrupts singular and stereotyped narratives. Through stories of lived experiences listeners/viewers of such stories have the opportunity to engage with a rich complexity of intersections between individual and shared values.

Oftentimes, the cross-current of individual experience and community reveals as much contradiction as they do similarities. For example, the performative narrative *Twilight-Los Angeles*, a play written and performed by Anna Deavere-Smith (1994), is committed to "a call to community, and a call to and an act of witnessing" (p. 10). In her performance, she reexamines the complex range of experiences narrated by those who witnessed the 1992 brutal assault of Rodney King and the ensuing uprising in Los Angeles following the acquittal of the police officers who beat him. As Giroux points out, "Deavere-Smith's reliance on excerpts and fragments additionally speaks to the need . . . (to) step back and ask whose perspectives, what perspectives, and what pieces of information are missing" (2013, p. 96). As a form of accomplicity, this process also includes a call for collective action, which "can therefore provide background knowledge for students to use in conjunction with understandings gleaned through the autobiographics to affect change" (Smith, 2013, p. 6).

Duoethnography

Another mode of inquiry suited for a curriculum of accomplicity is duoethnography (Hummel & Toyosaki, 2015; Sawyer & Norris, 2012). Duoethnography is based on four tenets: (a) it remains open-ended, (b) each voice remains explicit, (c) change of perspective is central, and (d) differences in point of view are its strength. Duoethnography is embedded in two narrative research traditions: storytelling and *currere* (Wallace & Byers, 2018). Indeed, *currere* is a "foundational tenet" (Norris & Sawyer, 2017, p. 2) of the duoethnographic process.

What makes duoethnography unique is the deliberately dialogic aspect, focusing on two voices with divergent experiences (or recollections) with a particular subject without privileging one voice over the other.

The hegemonic inclinations toward meta-narrative found in collaborative autoethnography are avoided by critically juxtaposing the stories of two different individuals who experience a similar phenomenon. This polyvocal storytelling to storytelling uses contrasting narratives and engaging in dialogue with/among each other as a means to dismantle the systems and processes of power and privilege that sustain uncertainty. The dialogue itself transforms the act of remembering or interrogating oneself. This process creates cracks and juxtapositions between identities and perceptions of events. Duoethnography is an effective approach for accomplice-inquiry in that the self is both the topic and yet not the center of the inquiry. Self is not a fixed entity but a fluid one, and the construction of self is contingent on its relationship with another.

Arts-Based Inquiry

All art forms are modes of communication, and as such have the potential to express critical sociopolitical ideas, such as the Radical Black Art movement (See Kelly, 2003). However, we must not romanticize art as possessing magical powers or being inherently liberatory. The processes of arts-based inquiry are not without their limitations. I concur with the argument made by Gaztambide-Fernández that "art does not change anything" (2009, p. 78). What I do suggest is the *possibility* of art, given its context, such as that of an accomplicity framework, to disrupt dominant narratives, question events, and create spaces for agency. Educators are encouraged to see themselves as public intellectuals (Willinsky, 2011) by making their work more public.

One example of arts-based inquiry as testimony is the artwork of Bearing Witness (2021) by the Hamilton Arts Collective in Baltimore, Maryland, which focused on how events of 2020 affected the artists. Works include Pete Stern's *Brush Fire*, which embodies the artist's reaction to the terrible fires in Australia in 2020. His work entitled *Support* conveys "the love and support from friends and family in the time of COVID-19 isolation" (personal communication, February 2021). His other painting, *Assault*, is "based on the recent attack on our nation's capital" (personal communication, February 2021).

CHALLENGES AND FUTURE DIRECTIONS

The goal of embracing a curriculum of accomplicity is not "triumph over difference" (Strauss, 1999, p. 45). Accomplicity means moving beyond the well-worn liberal trope echoed by generations of teachers who claim that "they don't see color," even as a well-intended attempt to treat all students equally. A curriculum of accomplicity requires a teacher to embrace their discomfort, dislocate their privilege, and focus on White privilege while acknowledging the collective harm that centuries of privilege have done (Apol, 2021). Active witnessing, empathetic listening, repositioning one's privilege—and all of the other actions outlined here—require an ongoing process of trial and error. The accomplice is never finished learning, and one must expect mis-steps and mistakes along the way. Knowledge is always partial and the work is always evolving.

A Word about Indigenous Methodologies

The challenges to being an accomplice are many, and the outline (figure 7.1) explored in this chapter is not devoid of problems. One issue that warrants exploration beyond the scope of this chapter is the question of representation in inquiry. Inquiry leads to knowledge production used in democratic spaces which, if left unquestioned, can reproduce the same White-centered narratives such democratic spaces claim to disrupt. I advocate for questioning the content of curricula and pedagogical practices, but so must there also be a continuous critical examination of the methods of inquiry used to examine those curricular and pedagogical practices. Beyond the examples of inquiry methods summarized here, it is important to recognize the vast array of significant Indigenous methodologies, which are too many, and too complex and rich in history to be justly described within the scope of this chapter.

In brief, "Indigenous methodologies and methods have become both systems for generating knowledge and ways of responding to the processes of colonization" (Evans et al., 2014, p. 180). I suggest, however, that any accomplicity curriculum includes the roles and relationships an accomplice may develop with Indigenous inquiry. Understanding that Whiteness and privilege do not entitle everyone to participate in every inquiry method[5] because "very specific Indigenous methods emerge from language, culture, and worldview" (p. 180). The central issue is assuring Indigenous knowledge is credited to Indigenous Peoples when used by other researchers in order to diminish the rising tide of erasure in Indigenous Studies. Scholarship, like land, is often commodified, colonized, or gentrified by White liberals when left unchecked.

CONCLUSION

The physical (and intellectual) self are repositioned to avert revisionist history, and instead engages with a revised understanding of the self. To witness, as a praxis, is to transmute the discomfort and pain of the marginalized to the pain and discomfort of Whiteness. Strauss (1999) contends that "outward political changes without inner transformation of the individual, would only lead to shifts in power from one group to another" (pp. 135–136). The accomplice must strive to work beyond the colonized mind and systems of language, power, and identity without knowing what place or role that might lead them to. That is because "knowing from the margins is inextricably linked to but distinct from knowing from the privileged space of the center" (Edgerton, 1996 as cited in Baszile, 2015, p. 122).

The purpose of the curriculum of accomplicity explored here is to clarify the contradictions and complexities embedded in our educational systems. First, we need to develop a politics of imagination (Desai, 2009) that enables us to reimagine power and ask critical questions that lead to alternative futures, for schools and communities. Second, we must be ever aware of the "tension between concerns over a racialized solipsism and the rejoinder that arguing against autobiography is akin to catering to the power relations that the critics are trying to avoid" (Smith, 2013, p. 6), in order to remain "self-reflective, progressive and critically cognizant" (p. 6). Most importantly, this chapter avoids overgeneralizations such as that there exists a singular Black historical narrative. Instead, I argue that a curriculum of accomplicity "antagonizes many of these assumptions by considering intergenerational factors within Black narratives to offer greater nuance and complexity" (Vandiver & Wiggen, 2021, p. 13). To practice accomplicity is to elevate the facets of a shared racialized experience living with/through an oppressive system but to do so without essentializing any position or narrative of marginalized peoples (Baszile, 2015). We must work to rearrange White privilege, rather than allowing unchecked White privilege to rearrange history. It is necessary to simultaneously own and dislocate one's Whiteness, to remain uncomfortable. I conclude this chapter with the words of Malcolm X (in Bailey, 2020) who says White people

> should be out on the battle line where America's racism really is—and that's in their own communities.... I tell sincere White people "work in conjunction with us—each of us work among our own kind." Let sincere White individuals find all other White people they can who feel as they do—and let them form their own all-white groups to try to convert other White people who are acting so racist. Let sincere White people teach non-violence to White people. (para. 5)

NOTES

1. In this chapter, the "W" in "White" is capitalized when addressing race following Nguyễn and Pendleton's (2020) recommendations.
2. The author identifies as a White middle-class and middle-aged heterosexual woman.
3. In this chapter, the action of *decolonize* refers to "decentralizing power . . . it's about centering the very groups of people most vulnerable to the oppression of colonization . . . using colonial tools to defend ourselves seems like an inevitable metamorphosis into a tool of the colonizer" (Yasmeen Mjalli, 2020, para 7).
4. *Radical* is defined in Webster's Dictionary as "advocating or based on thorough or complete political or social change; relating to or affecting the fundamental nature of something."
5. Cora Weber-Pillwax (1999) distinguishes between Indigenous research methodology that may be selected as a methodology by all researchers and Indigenous research conducted by Indigenous scholars.

REFERENCES

Adorno, T. (1998). The meaning of working through the past (Trans. H Pickford). In *Critical models: Interventions and catchwords* (pp. 89–104). Columbia University Press.
Apol, L. (2021). *Poetry, poetic inquiry and Rwanda: Engaging with the lives of others*. Springer.
Anthropocene Curriculum. (2021). About. https://www.anthropocene-curriculum.org/about
Applebaum, B. (2010). *Being White, being good: White complicity, white moral responsibility, and social justice pedagogy*. Lexington Books.
Bailey, P. (2020). Bailey: Brother Malcolm's message to 'Sincere Whites.' https://www.washingtoninformer.com/bailey-brother-malcolms-message-to-sincere-whites/
Baszile, D. (2015). Critical race/feminist currere. In B. Schultz & W. Schubert (Eds.), *The Sage guide to curriculum in education* (pp. 119–126). Sage Publications. https://www.doi.org/10.4135/9781483346687.n19
Bearing Witness. (2021). [art exhibit]. Hamilton Art Collective. https://hamiltonarts.org/bearingwitness/
Britzman, D. (2000). If the story cannot end: Deferred action, ambivalence, and difficult knowledge. In R. I. Simon, S. Rosenberg, & C. Eppert (Eds.), *Between hope and despair: Pedagogy and the remembering of historical trauma* (pp. 27–58). Rowman & Littlefield.
Britzman, D. (2014). Thoughts on the fragility of peace. *LLinE Journal*, 2. http://www.lline.fi/en/issue/2_2014/issue-22014
Chalmers, D. (2010). *The character of consciousness*. Oxford University Press.

Chaturvedi, M. (2015). Ethical witnessing: The poetics and politics of testimony. In P. Morgan (Ed.), *The arc of memory in the aftermath of trauma* (pp. 1–10). Brill/Sense.

Clifford, P., Friesen, S., & Jardine, C. (2001). Whatever happens to him happens to us: Reading coyote reading the world. *Journal of Educational Thought, 35*(1), 9–26.

Daspit, T., & McDermott, M. (1990). Frameworks of blood and bone: An alchemy of performative mapping. In C. Bagley & M. Cancienne (Eds.), *Dancing the data* (pp. 51–74). Peter Lang.

Deavere-Smith, A. (1994). *Twilight: Los Angeles, 1992.* Anchor Books.

Desai, D. (2009). Imagining justice in times of perpetual war: Notes for the classroom. *Journal of Curriculum and Pedagogy, 6*(2), 6–26.

Ellsworth, E. (2005). *Places of learning: Media, architecture, pedagogy.* Routledge.

Evans, M., Miller, A., Hutchinson, P., & Dingwall, C. (2014). Decolonizing research practice. Indigenous methodologies, aboriginal methods, and knowledge/knowing. In P. Leavy (Ed.), *The Oxford handbook of qualitative research* (pp. 179–191). Oxford University Press.

Farley, L. (2009). Radical hope: Or the problem of uncertainty in history education. *Curriculum Inquiry, 39*(4), 537–554. https://doi.org/10.1111/j.1467-873X.2009.00456.x

Fine, M. (2006). Bearing witness: Methods for researching oppression and resistance—A textbook for critical research. *Social Justice Research, 19*(1), 83–108. https://doi.org/10.1007/s11211-006-0001-0

Gaztambide-Fernández, R. A. (2009). Toward creative solidarity in the "next" movement of curriculum work. In E. Malewski (Ed.), *Curriculum studies handbook: The next moment* (pp. 78–94). Routledge.

Giroux, C. (2013). *The traumatized/traumatizing subject in Anna Deavere Smith, Suzan-Lori Parks, And August Wilson* (Publication No. 881) [Doctoral dissertation, Wayne State University]. Digital Commons.

Harden, K., & Harden-Moore, T. (2019). Moving from ally to accomplice: How far are you willing to go to disrupt racism in the workplace? *Diverse Issues in Higher Education.* https://diverseeducation.com/article/138623/

Harjo, L. (2019). *Spiral to the stars: Mvskoke tools of futurity.* University of Arizona Press.

hooks, b. (1991). Theory as liberatory practice. *Yale Journal of Law and Feminism, 14*(12). https://digitalcommons.law.yale.edu/yjlf/vol4/iss1/2

hooks, b. (1994). *Teaching to transgress: Education as the practice of freedom.* Routledge Press.

Hummel, G. S., & Toyosaki, S. (2015). Duoethnography as relational whiteness pedagogy. *International Review of Qualitative Research, 8*(1), 27–48.

Hunn, L. R. M., Guy, T., & Mangliitz, E. (2006). *Who can speak for whom? Using counter-storytelling to challenge racial hegemony* [Paper presentation]. Adult Education Conference (AERC) 2006. https://newprairiepress.org/aerc/2006/papers/32

Indigenous Action Media. (2014). *Accomplices not allies: Abolishing the ally industrial complex.* https://www.indigenousaction.org/accomplices-not-allies-abolishing-the-ally-industrial-complex/comment-page-1/

Indigenous Action Media. (2015). Accomplices, not allies. In C. Milstein (Ed.), *Taking sides*, (pp. 85–97). AK Press.
Jackson, W. (2019). Don't be an ally, be an accomplice. https://forge.medium.com/dont-be-an-ally-be-an-accomplice-437869756ab5
Kelly, R. D. G. (2003). *Freedom dreams: The Black radical imagination*. Beacon Press.
Kumashiro, K. K. (2004). *Against common sense: Teaching and learning toward social justice*. Routledge.
Lewis-Beck, M. S., Bryman, A., & Futing Liao, T. (2004). *The SAGE encyclopedia of social science research methods*. Sage Publications. https://doi.org/10.4135/9781412950589
Marcus, G. (1997). The uses of complicity in the changing mise-en-scène of anthropological fieldwork. *Representations, 59*, 85–108. https://doi.org/10.2307/2928816
Milstein, C. (2015). Solidarity as weapon and practice, versus killer cops and white supremacy. In C. Milstein (Ed.), *Taking sides: Revolutionary solidarity and the poverty of liberalism* (pp. 137–150). AK Press.
Nguyễn, A. T., & Pendleton, M. (2020, March 23). Recognizing race in language: Why we capitalize "Black" and "White." *Center for the Study of Social Policy*. https://cssp.org/2020/03/recognizing-race-in-language-why-we-capitalize-black-and-white/
Norris, J., & Sawyer, R. (2017). *Theorizing curriculum studies, teacher education and research through duoethnographic pedagogy*. Springer.
Osler, J. (n.d.). Opportunities for White people in the fight for racial justice. *White Accomplices*. https://www.whiteaccomplices.org/
Pentón Herrera, L. J., & Obregón, N. (2020). Challenges facing Latinx ESOL students in the Trump era: Stories told through testimonios. *Journal of Latinos and Education, 19*(4), 383–391. https://doi.org/10.1080/15348431.2018.1523793
Pinar, W. F. (1978). *Currere*: A case study. In G. Willis (Ed.), *Qualitative evaluation: Concepts and cases in curriculum criticism* (pp. 316–342). McCutchan.
Pinar, W. F. (1994). Autobiography and an architecture of self. *Counterpoints, 2*, 201–222.
Powell, J., & Kelly, A. (2017). Accomplices in the academy in the age of Black Lives Matter. *Journal of Critical Thought and Praxis, 6*(2), 42–65. https://doi.org/10.31274/jctp-180810-73
Probyn-Rapsey, F. (2007). Complicity, critique and methodology. *ARIEL, 38* (2–3), 65–82.
Richardson, A. V. (2016). Bearing witness while Black: Theorizing African-American mobile journalism after Ferguson. *Digital Journalism, 5*(6), 673–698. https://doi.org/10.1080/21670811.2016.1193818
Rohr, R. (1989). *Breathing underwater: Spirituality and the 12 steps*. Franciscan Media.
Sandberg, C. (2013). *Lean in: Women, work and the will to lead*. Knopf.
Saunders, P. (2021, July 17). Attacks on critical race theory reopen old wounds. https://www.bloomberg.com/opinion/articles/2021-07-17/republican-critical-race-theory-attacks-exploit-democratic-divisions

Sawyer, R., & Norris, J. (2012). *Duoethnography: Understanding qualitative research*. Oxford University Press.

Sheridan, R. (2017). *Pedagogy of accomplice: Navigating complicity in pedagogies aimed toward social justice* (Publication No. 10169573) [Doctoral dissertation, Southern Illinois University Carbondale]. Open SIUC.

Smith, B. (2013). Currere and critical pedagogy: Thinking critically about self-reflective methods. *Transnational Curriculum Inquiry, 10*(2), 3–16.

Strauss, D. L. (1999). *Between dog and wolf: Essays on art and politics*. Autonomedia Press.

Strauss, V. (2018, April 26). 'A Nation at Risk' demanded education reform 35 years ago. https://www.washingtonpost.com/news/answer-sheet/wp/2018/04/26/the-landmark-a-nation-at-risk-called-for-education-reform-35-years-ago-heres-how-it-was-bungled/

The Black Public Sphere Collective. (1995). *The black public sphere: A public culture book*. University of Chicago Press.

Tiger, T. (2015). Dangerous allies. In C. Milstein (Ed.), *Taking sides: Revolutionary solidarity and the poverty of liberalism* (pp. 48–63). AK Press.

Vandiver, M. J., & Wiggen, G. (2021). *The healing power of education. Afro-centric pedagogy as a tool for restoration and liberation*. Teachers College Press.

Wallace, M. F. G., & Byers, C. C. (2018). Duo-*Currere*: Nomads in dialogue (re)searching for possibilities of permeability in elementary science teacher education. *Currere Exchange Journal, 2*(1), 59–68.

Webb, L. (2004). "Testimonio", the assumption of hybridity and the issue of genre. *Studies in Testimony*. https://studiesintestimony.co.uk/issues/volume-two-issue-one-2019/testimonio-the-assumption-of-hybridity-and-the-issue-of-genre/

Will, M. (2019). Bearing witness to "White Supremacy" one meal at a time. *Front Porch*. https://frontporchne.com/article/bearing-witness-white-supremacy-one-meal-time/

Willinsky, J. (2011). How to be more of a public intellectual by making your intellectual work more public. *Journal of Curriculum and Pedagogy, 3*(1), 92–95. https://doi.org/10.1080/15505170.2006.10411583

Zembylas, M. (2014). Theorizing "difficult knowledge" in the aftermath of the "affective turn": Implications for curriculum and pedagogy in handling traumatic representations. *Curriculum Inquiry, 44*(3), 390–412. https://doi.org/10.111/curi/12051

Chapter 8

Combating Anti-Asian Bias by Developing Intercultural Maturity through a Short-Term Study Abroad Program in China

Ashley Lucas and Xiaoming Liu

This chapter intends to combat the increasing anti-Asian racism and xenophobia by sharing university students' firsthand experience in a short-term study abroad (STSA) program in China. Students' development in intercultural maturity (ICM) (Perez et al., 2015) is analyzed to demonstrate how some of their pre-held bias and stereotypes toward China were broken from having the immersion experience and through utilizing ethical frameworks when considering social issues. We argue that ICM lays the foundation for being antiracist, and a well-designed study abroad trip can be a strategy to prepare antiracist teachers. We also discuss challenges we have encountered and provide suggestions with regard to how to move forward with a successful antiracist and antibias teacher education.

INTRODUCTION

Discrimination against China and the Chinese American community has increased with the outbreak of COVID-19. According to a national report released by Stop Asian Americans and Pacific Islanders Hate (Jeung et al., 2021), 6,603 incidents were reported from March 19, 2020, to March 31, 2021, among which "Chinese individuals reported more hate incidents (43.7%) than other race or ethnic groups, followed by Koreans (16.6%), Filipinx (8.8%) and Vietnamese (8.3%)" (p. 1). The COVID-19 virus was first identified in Wuhan, China, and has been repeatedly called the "China Virus" or "Wuhan Virus" by certain media, politicians, and individuals.

Unfortunately, anti-Chinese sentiment in the United States is not a new phenomenon.

Historically, Chinese Americans have been stigmatized as perpetual foreigners (Lee et al., 2009), disease carriers (Eichelberger, 2007), and filthy or dirty (Lee, 2017). Xenophobia and anti-Asian rhetoric resurged upon the outbreak of the COVID-19 virus, including misleading information and videos that have gone viral on the Internet. False information on the media about certain racial or ethnic groups can perpetuate fear and continue to fuel racial discrimination during a pandemic (Wen et al., 2020). As educators, we feel obligated to combat the resurgence of anti-Asian racism and xenophobia through disseminating what our students saw, heard, and experienced during a STSA program in China. Thus, in this chapter, we present and report findings from a qualitative study that took place in 2016.

Even though this STSA trip occurred before the pandemic, we hope that our participants' firsthand experience will be informative to the educational community. The purposes of this chapter are twofold: First, we share our students' cognitive, intrapersonal, and interpersonal journey toward developing ICM at different points throughout the STSA program in China. Their development toward ICM illustrates how some of their pre-held bias and stereotypes were broken by being in the country and utilizing ethical frameworks when analyzing social issues. We argue that study abroad trips, if well designed, can be a strategy to prepare antiracist teachers. Second, this chapter introduces China from the eyes of our participants. Their firsthand experience may be educational to the general public, especially those who are not familiar with the country.

CONTEXT

As our nation and K–12 schools become more diverse, it is essential that teachers, who the majority continue to be White and female, can work and understand children from all backgrounds (Ladson-Billings, 2014; Sleeter & Thao, 2007). Teachers need to be able to "recognize various opinions and practices and see further than one's own perspective on politics, ethnics, religious, and national views" (Cox, 1991, as cited in Clarke et al., 2009, p. 174) and to be not only culturally responsive but antiracist as well. Advocates argue that study abroad programs are able to achieve this goal (Cushner & Chang, 2015).

The qualitative study abroad program described in this chapter provided participants an immersion experience where they constantly negotiated with themselves cognitively, intrapersonally, and interpersonally while developing ICM (Perez et al., 2015) in an unfamiliar and different cultural environment.

We also implemented ethical frameworks in the program to offer our students alternative frames of reference when considering social issues. As a result, most of the participants gained renewed perspectives and perceptions of China and became more interculturally mature. ICM enables individuals to understand the complexities of intercultural issues (Bennett & Bennett, 2004; Perez et al., 2015) and be more culturally sensitive.

THEORETICAL PERSPECTIVE

In this chapter, we emphasize participants' learning outcomes in areas including Chinese culture, education, and ethical issues and connect the outcomes to the developmental model of ICM (Perez et al., 2015). This widely used model seeks to examine how individuals understand complex intercultural issues and act in culturally and contextually appropriate ways. We also explore how bringing in ethical frameworks can be a conduit in helping to deepen ICM.

Perez et al. (2015) refined and expanded on King and Baxter Magolda's (2005) developmental model of ICM. The model considers how individuals (a) understand cultural differences (cognitive dimensions), (b) accept and appreciate cultural differences (intrapersonal dimensions), and (c) interact with those of cultural differences (interpersonal dimension). Table 8.1 provides a brief description of the various levels of ICM based on Perez et al.'s 2015 version. By considering how individuals grapple with cognitive, intrapersonal, and interpersonal domains of development, the model helps to gauge the level at which individuals develop ICM.

This chapter also explores how applying ethical frameworks, particularly those of consequentialism and non-consequentialism, can potentially be utilized as a powerful aid in developing ICM. Consequentialism is often connected with philosophers such as Jeremy Bentham (utilitarianism) and John Stuart Mill. There are many branches and subsets of consequentialism, but simply put, it is the idea that one makes decisions based on the greatest good for the greatest number of people (see Shackleton, 1972). In connection to this idea is the concept of benefit maximization, which is often described as the overall balance of pleasure over pain. The right thing to do is whatever will maximize utility, which produces pleasure or happiness, and whatever prevents pain or suffering. Non-consequentialism is most often associated with Immanuel Kant. Kant and other non-consequentialist are concerned not with numbers and consequences but with the notion of natural rights (see Krieger, 1965). As Sandel (2009) emphasized, "If all human beings are worthy of respect, regardless of who they are or where they live, then it's wrong to treat them as mere instruments of the collective happiness" (p. 103).

Table 8.1 Development Model of Intercultural Maturity

	Cognitive	Intrapersonal	Interpersonal
Initial	Culture is viewed in simplistic terms where different perspectives are considered as wrong. Unable to consider variation within groups.	Take one's identity for granted. Does not understand the complexities of the intersection of social identity.	Reluctant to interact with others who are viewed as different. Fails to understand the impact of social systems on group norms and intergroup.
Intermediate	Different perspectives are viewed as valid and are placed within historical and political contexts. Begins to be aware and accepts multiple perspectives.	Acknowledges legitimacy of other cultures. Considers identity within broader social contexts.	Willing to interact with others who are viewed as different. Begins to understand the impact of social systems affecting group norms.
Mature	Consciously uses multiple cultural frameworks to consider alternative perspectives and behaviors.	Open to coalition building in a global and national context. Willing to challenge one's views and perspectives.	Capable of engaging in meaningful relationships with others. Shows appreciation of differences and willing to challenge oppressive social situations.

RESEARCH BASE

There has been significant research on the positive effects of study abroad on participants' development of cross-cultural understanding and transformative thinking. This line of research has crossed a range of fields and lengths of programs (Blake-Campbell, 2014; Hutchison & Rea, 2011; Ritz, 2011; Vatalaro et al., 2015; Walters et al., 2017). For example, Gambino and Hashim (2016) argue that high-quality programs can lead to experiences where participants not only deepen their cross-cultural understandings but are able to increase their understanding of themselves as global citizens with responsibilities.

However, over the years, there has been backlash as to whether study abroad, in general, truly leads to cross-cultural understanding, or if it is simply assumed that it is beneficial without providing evidence (Engle, 2013; Sachau et al., 2009; Terzuolo, 2018). Some argue that the longer the exposure, the more learning occurs (DeLoach et al., 2021). Others, such as Paige et al.'s (2009) study surveying the data of over 6,000 alumni stretching over 20 universities, found no significant difference in those who studied abroad long term and those who spent a few weeks.

As Wilson (1982) reflected, "A summer trip to Europe does not necessarily a global perspective. Persons are more likely to "learn from experience when they are prepared for the experience, engage in educational activities during the experience, and evaluate the experience" (p. 185). Research by Vande Berg (2014), Spencer and Tuma (2002), and Cushner and Chang (2015) emphasized that study abroad itself is not sufficient to bring about change in intercultural competence. They stressed that study abroad experiences need to be carefully crafted to bring about changes in frames and intercultural learning. To make these programs even more transformative, Gaia (2015) advocates that programs need to seek ways to increase awareness of the complexity of various cultures and their own responsibility as global citizens.

Donnelly-Smith (2009) argues that STSA programs have the added benefit of most programs being faculty led, which allows faculty to have more control over the program and better integrate course content and activities. Other researchers also emphasized the importance of predeparture training on cross-cultural experiences (Brislin & Kim, 2003; Gao & Gudykunst, 1990) and ample opportunities for critical reflections throughout the trip (Husu et al., 2008). Vande Berg (2014) argues that immersive experiences should happen within the context of reflections and discussion so that students can develop their intercultural identity.

Though there have been studies that demonstrate an increase in ICM and transformative learning, none of the existing literature found focuses on using ethical frameworks as tools to facilitate students' transformation. Our qualitative study intends to fill the gap. Hill (2005) ascertained that "ethics really begins when my moral context collides with the moral contexts of others, pulling me in new directions. It implies a continual stretching beyond parochial political, economic, and cultural loyalties" (p. 223). As with Hoggan and Cranton's (2015) work centering on university students, we suggest that there is the potential that utilizing ethical frameworks can be a catalyst in three areas they describe: creating a disorienting dilemma, leading to critical reflection, or looking at oneself or the world through a new lens.

ANTIRACIST TEACHER EDUCATION PRACTICE AND IMPLEMENTATION

Our STSA program was embedded within a course entitled *Education and Ethics in the Land of Confucius*. This course was designed and co-led by two university faculty members in the college of education from a mid-Atlantic state university. The authors adapted an existing core course on ethics in education to one that looked specifically at ethics and education in China. The main goal for this course was to help students become open-minded, empathetic, and see the beauty of difference, all of which helps one to work toward becoming antiracist. We aimed to offer students an international experience to provide them with a lens to look at issues of education and ethics comparatively, reflectively, and critically. In particular, we emphasized using ethical frameworks to examine educational and societal issues. Donnelly-Smith's (2009) five best practices for STSA guided the design of the program: strong, clear academic content; faculty that are comfortable and competent; integration with the local community; lecturers from the host country; and requiring ongoing reflection individually and as a group.

The predeparture section of the program lasted two weeks and was conducted through an online learning platform. Students read about and studied various topics, including Chinese culture, education, history, and philosophy, as well as various ethical frameworks, such as consequentialism, non-consequentialism, utilitarianism, ethics of care, equal opportunity, and democratic freedom. Students were also asked to write a pre-trip paper on their initial perceptions, thoughts, feelings, and beliefs regarding China. Particular attention was paid to issues of ethics and social justice.

The in-country portion of the program was two weeks, divided among three cities: Qingdao, Qufu, and Beijing. As instructors, we were mindful that we needed to structure our program in a way that provides meaningful educational opportunities for our students rather than merely sightseeing tours. The trip consisted of discussion forums led by the professors, lectures by local guest speakers, and field experiences. During the field experiences, students visited three public schools covering diverse levels (elementary, middle, and high school levels), one School for the Deaf in Qingdao, and one university in Beijing, along with various cultural excursions in all cities. Students had plentiful opportunities throughout the trip to interact with local people: school children, teachers, university students, guest lecturers, and tour guides. Students documented their daily experiences through journaling. Upon return, they completed a post-trip analysis paper. Students were also interviewed a semester after they returned to the United States when they would have 'calmed down' from the excitement of the trip.

METHODOLOGY

This is an event case study (Yin, 2018) aiming to investigate the effect of a STSA trip in China on a group of college students. A total of seven students participated in this program, all identified as females. None of them had been to China before. Table 8.2 summarizes their educational backgrounds.

Data collected for this study include (a) pre-trip paper, (b) journal entries, (c) post-trip paper, (d) analysis paper, and (e) interviews (one semi-structured interview to one student who could not join the small-group interview, and one small-group interview with the other seven students). The pre-trip paper asked students to write about their initial perceptions, thoughts, feelings, and beliefs regarding China with particular attention to issues of ethics and social justice. For the journal entries, we requested students to write daily observations of the various field experiences in China, such as school visits, excursions, interactions, and communications and reflect on them. The post-trip analysis paper asked students to compare their initial ideas about China in terms of cultural competences, ethics, and social justice with what they had observed and experienced on the trip and how it might affect their future professional roles.

In the analysis paper, students chose a topic relevant to either or both countries and analyzed the topic from multiple perspectives including different ethical frameworks. All students participated in the interviews. We conducted one individual semi-structured interview and one small-group interview with the rest of the students based on their work and study schedules. The semi-structured interviews intended to seek their reflection on how the trip had affected their personal and professional growth. Some interview questions include: Do you think your thinking about China changed during the trip? Has the trip affected the way you think about people, events, and ethical issues? How do you think the trip might guide your future professional decisions?

Analytic induction was used to review the data to identify basic themes. The themes were refined after further analysis and connected to the literature.

Table 8.2 Participants

Name (pseudonyms)	Year	Major
Amy	Graduate	Master of Arts in Teaching
Camille	Junior	Speech pathology
Sadie	Freshman	Science (teaching certification)
Kiara	Senior	Dance
Jessica	Junior	Pre-early childhood
Leah	Junior	Special education
Fiona	Junior	Secondary Education

We analyzed the data according to whether the students were engaging in anything that looked like there was potential for intercultural development. We paid particular attention to whether they applied consequentialist and non-consequentialist frameworks.

REFLECTION ON EFFECTIVENESS OF PRACTICE

Analyzing before and after changes helps us to consider whether an STSA program can aid preservice teachers to become antiracists. Several themes emerged from the data that include the importance of visiting multiple locations and carefully designing an STSA program, how utilizing ethical frameworks can lead to ICM development, and how an STSA program can counter misinformation from the media.

Importance of Visiting Multiple Locations

School visits were an essential component of this study abroad program. As our students visited more schools, their understanding of China's education broadened. The first school was a high school located in a rural area outside Qingdao City that has a very high college acceptance rate. Students in this school have long study hours under the pressure of China's college entrance exam. Upon leaving the school, our students commented that China put too much emphasis on academics, and they felt sad to see children had to spend so much time on school and missed out on a lot of other things in life. Kiara expressed:

> I definitely was alarmed by the emphasis to meet a certain standard in China. There is so much pressure on the children to succeed academically that it seems that it would be overwhelming. They do not have the luxury to come home and play videogames and then start on their homework. Since they get home so late, the only thing they have time to do is do their homework and get some more studying done.

It is clear the students were at the initial stage of the cognitive domain as they regarded different cultural phenomena as strange.

The following day, we visited a middle school and an elementary school, both located in an affluent neighborhood of Qingdao City. Participants' perceptions of Chinese schools changed as shown in their journal entries. Leah wrote, "After going to the high school the previous day which showed a one-way street to success, it was nice to see how much the other schools were trying to promote creativity and culture." Amy remarked:

Visiting the elementary and middle schools today helped change my perspective on education in China. I was very surprised at the emphasis on humanities at both schools. After seeing the high school yesterday, I was expecting the elementary and middle schools to be much more test-driven rather than creativity-driven. While the elementary and middle school may [be] individual cases, it was still something that I was not expecting to see after reading the articles prior to coming to China, as well as visiting the high school.

Jessica commented after visiting the elementary school, "I was very surprised by this school because it emphasized the humanities, whereas I had this preconceived notion that all schools were like little boot camps for learning, where it was only math and sciences that were focused on." Participants' change in perception from one day to the next indicates the importance of including multiple types of schools and locations in a study abroad program. Lack of variety could lead to a one-sided view of a certain phenomenon. We are fully aware that a visit to three cities is not representative of all of China. We selected, however, three cities that would provide diverse experiences in a short period of time.

As the participants became more interculturally mature, they began to consider how what they witnessed in the schools in China could inform their teaching in the United States. Fiona took note of the lecture-style instructional method she observed in the high school and said if she has students who have been raised in China, she would explain to these students there is a participation grade in her class and "it's okay to call out or answer questions out loud . . . just keeping in mind the ways that kids learn at home and how that's going to make them learn differently in my classroom." For Amy, even though she did not think the extremely competitive environment in the high school was healthy, she acknowledged the cultural differences. Further, the diligence she saw from the Chinese children inspired her to encourage her own students to work even harder. She stated:

> One thing that is very evident is that children are capable of doing a lot more than we give them credit for in the United States. I do not think forcing them to go to school for 12 hours a day is healthy or appropriate. . . . However, the children do the work and push themselves. I think there is something to this. The motivation that inspires these children to work and excel is something to achieve in my own classroom.

Fiona and Amy demonstrated that they were becoming more open-minded and culturally conscious. Researchers believe that increased level of self-reflectiveness and cultural sensitivity equips preservice teachers to be less ethnocentric and more capable of teaching the ever-changing student

Careful Design of Progress

It is evident that our participants' development toward ICM was mostly at the initial level during the beginning of the trip. The trajectory moved toward the mature level near the end of the trip. Heavily influenced by the media, their pre-trip perceptions about China included strictness in many different facets of life, including school, government censorship, constraint of the freedom of religion, and the one-child policy. At the beginning of the trip, especially after visiting the high school and the School for the Deaf in Qingdao, many participants used the frame of reference that they were most familiar with (i.e., their personal experience) to judge these schools instead of putting a cultural phenomenon in its context. Take the School for the Deaf, for example, from observation and discussions with the teachers, we learned that this school strived to encourage the students to use their voice, which is not the practice in the United States. Some students deemed that the country's special education system is backward based on merely one school visit. Sadie wrote, "It was almost sad to learn how far behind the system here supposedly is." Similarly, Jessica commented, "It was clear to see that their deaf education is farther behind the United States' deaf education. From that, I got the impression that the entire special education system was farther behind, due to the emphasis on perfection in their society."

However, we noted more incidents at the mature level toward the end of the trip, as some participants were able to use multiple cultural frames when analyzing educational and social issues. In Leah's final paper, she emphasized perspective. She referred to the visit of the School for the Deaf and commented that other students' criticism of the oral-based learning system was incorrect because they failed to consider China's culture and perspective. Sadie expressed a similar perspective when she noted, ". . . really realizing that you can have a truth, someone else can have a truth, and they can both be true because they are coming from different perspectives and different places. Just because they are not exactly the same doesn't mean one of them is necessarily wrong or untrue."

The fact that our students progressively gained more ICM may be attributed to the careful design of the program. Throughout the trip, we provided ample opportunities for our participants to interact with the local community, including small-group conversations with teachers and administrators, one-on-one discussions with K–12 school children and college students, as well as continuous interaction with our tour guide who traveled with us the entire time. Research indicates that students tend to get the most out of an STSA

Ethical Frameworks

While we speculated that activities such as going to schools and talking to people would influence students' level of ICM, we were struck by how ethical frameworks provided a tool for students to analyze and discover the nuances of complex issues. Amy, Fiona, and Sadie were particularly astute in bringing in ethical frameworks in their understanding of policy differences. They all made the connection between non-consequentialism and the U.S. promotion of human rights and support for the individual. Conversely, they applied a consequentialist framework to China's advancement of itself as a country for its people by supporting the national population above all else.

This application of ethical frameworks helped them develop new frames of reference. Amy's changing worldview became apparent when she considered in her final paper how, as a U.S. citizen, she supports individual rights. However, "after visiting China and learning about their culture, history, and life, I am not sure if the U.S. ideals would suit China. China's population is almost triple the size of the U.S." She further writes that China is committed to benefiting maximization with the greatest benefit for the most people and how it connects to China's beliefs, religion, and culture. By having this new frame of reference, Amy was able to engage in a deeper understanding of China and its policies. It was not an embrace of policy, but a more thoughtful understanding of it. Similarly, Sadie demonstrated a mature level of thinking when she advocated that the United States and China could learn from each other. She wrote:

> Students' inability to choose a major in college has led to a balanced workforce without shortage [in China]. The common man's inability to own guns has led to police officers not wearing them on duty [in China] and a lower murder rate than the U.S. These differences in opinion may have long caused the two countries to clash, but, in reality, they have a lot to learn from one another.

The most apparent aspect of students' utilizing ethical frameworks was students' discussion about China's one-child policy. When discussing China's one-child policy, Fiona, Sadie, and Amy put it in the context of China's traditional values—community betterment before individual benefits. Amy acknowledged that had some of these policies not been put into practice, there would be famine and that uncontrolled population would overwhelm services, such as education and healthcare. Sadie wrote:

I remember learning about it when I was a child and being abhorred that such a law could exist anywhere in the world. I believed that such a rule was inhumane and just plain wrong. As I've grown older, however, and learned more about our environment and other reasons behind the law, it seems to make more sense. . . . In my mind, it seems to make logical sense, even if I'm not really sure how I stand on the matter ethically.

In her final paper, Sadie analyzed the one-child policy through the lens of consequentialism and non-consequentialism. She discussed how China's laws are more in line with consequentialism, which leads to policies that are aimed

for the betterment of the country, occasionally at the loss of individual rights. The one and two child policies are an excellent example of this. Here, the country recognized its need to slow the population or else face drastic results, such as famine, at the national level, so it removed reproductive rights from its citizens.

Sadie went on to write:

In China, women can be sterilized for having an extra child without a permit, but in the U.S., there is an overabundance of unemployed families with multiple children on the street. . . . Both countries obviously have either ethical or economic issues challenging them as a result of their ideology. To solve issues such as the world population rate, greenhouse emissions, and space exploration, we are going to need to learn to work together and compromise.

Fiona and others also brought up several times how critical it is to have firsthand accounts about issues such as the one-child policy and how they play a role in group norms. Utilizing ethical frameworks appears to have facilitated intercultural competence and maturity by providing the scaffolding that Perez et al. (2015) suggest.

Not everyone mentioned ethical frameworks in their final papers. This absence was most noticeably in Camille's remarks:

While American society would never allow the government to regulate something as personal as the number of children born to a family, China's society first mindset made these things acceptable in the eyes of the public. In America, the thought of someone being forced into sterilization by the government would cause riots, but in China, it was seen as a way to punish someone who broke the law by having a second child. While I don't agree with this disregard for natural human rights, I grew up outside Chinese culture and do not understand how society could allow that kind of government control.

She acknowledges that she grew up outside Chinese culture, but her thinking on the topic appears linear.

Media versus Reality

Our students drew a comparison between what they actually experienced in China and what they had known about it prior to the trip. For example, in terms of the environment, Amy suggested that the United States gives a less than honest portrayal of China's pollution. She praised the beauty of Qingdao and claimed the water was cleaner than on the U.S. East Coast. It is noted that this was written before the group traveled to Beijing where they experienced dense smog. They realized, however, that not all of China is riddled with pollution.

Amy later admitted that she had a "Disney" picture of China. Instead, she noted that China is modern. Sadie claimed, "Before, I was thinking the Great Wall, pandas, and [I had a] negative connotation because of a lot of strange laws that we are not used to here. Actually, going there, talking to people, realizing how similar people are, it came to life. These are real people. This is a real place."

With regard to the government, Sadie wrote in her journals how she had been misinformed about China. In her early reflections she wrote:

> Under no circumstances should people be put down for a way of thinking. Whether it be curiosity which drives someone to Google, or a deeply held religious belief which drives someone to practice in their home, thoughts and ideas cannot and should not be put down. I believe this to be my main problem with Chinese law currently.

She wrote that when she was young her youth group at church taught her that all religious practices were not sanctioned by the Chinese government, and people were arrested for practicing Christianity in their homes. She acknowledged that "Now, I've learned that this is not entirely true nor entirely false." Later Sadie stated in the interview, "The only thing we hear about China is from the news—always about this overpowering government, bad communism, blah blah. So, you go there, you think it is going to be so depressive ... upset and so sad with their lives. When you get there, you are like '*really*'?" However, Camille seemed to have a different view. She wrote about her frustration with censorship that she felt was rampant:

> Throughout our trip, it was more inconvenient than infuriating that we were unable to access Facebook, Gmail, Instagram, Twitter, and numerous other popular American websites. I did not see a direct problem with government

censorship of social media, but more with the news itself. Fiona and I watched the news in English when we were in Qufu. The praise given to Chinese officials and new policies as well as the look on other societies was almost laughable. No government is as perfect as that newscaster made China look. Every country has some degree of government censorship of the media, but it appeared that China had more.

Camille appears unable to move forward. While she acknowledges that every country has some censorship, she found the praise of officials "laughable." Sadie brought up the idea of suppression of religion by the government. Throughout the trip, there were several visits to religious centers—a Catholic Church, a Daoist temple, and several Buddhist temples. Particularly informative was spending several hours in a Buddhist temple complex guided by two Buddhist monks. In her final paper, Sadie wrote how our guide and others indicated that religious suppression was not as big of a deal as the media makes it out to be.[1] During the post-trip interview, Sadie voiced that the negative connotations related to China that she received prior to the trip did not turn out to be true. Jessica also articulated many facets of Chinese culture and life that are like her own. Fiona said, "China has a negative connotation. . . . Being able to go, I didn't notice. Obviously, we didn't live there, we didn't have to feel the government, the power."

MOVING FORWARD

Ignorance and assumptions often fuel racist attitudes. One way to counter racism is to gain firsthand experience to understand a community better. Experiences can be so much more powerful than a book or article. The challenge becomes determining what experiences during study abroad are valuable in promoting ICM. Study abroad programs need to go beyond being simply 'cool' trips. Ideally, they should prepare students to become interculturally competent and widen their worldview. As Cushner and Chang (2015) write, "It is the acquisition of intercultural competence, and not knowledge alone, that will be essential" (p. 167). This, however, does not happen automatically. Therefore, a significant question related to this is how instructors on study abroad trips can assist learners in becoming aware and critical of assumptions. One exciting development that seemed to occur through interacting with local people (students, teachers, and our tour guide) and visiting multiple locations is that it opened a window for understanding individual and community practices and an appreciation for a diversity of ideas.

In the case of this course, having first-person experiences was a critical step to developing antiracist attitude. Having students consider what they saw, read about, and experienced through ethical frameworks helped to further develop their thinking and ICM level. These first-person experiences, in turn, helped them move forward to becoming antiracists by being more open-minded and cognizant of the validity of the portrayal of China in the media. ICM lays the foundation for being antiracist. We could have done more, however, to both stress ethical frameworks and debrief their reflections to encourage their further development of ICM. Analyzing the writings of our students revealed that not all students had a solid grasp of the ethical frameworks themselves. Comprehending and applying ethical frameworks to situations can be tricky. While some of the students were able to make the leap of applying ethical frameworks to issues, not all students did or with as much finesse. Moving forward, we would spend more time making certain that all students have a clear understanding of the ethical frameworks and give them more practice applying them to scenarios. Additionally, while we had students reflect in their journals, we believe that having more formal debriefing sessions and sharing of journal reflections would be beneficial.

More updated and targeted readings on antiracism, colonialism, and history of discrimination of Chinese and Chinese Americans are needed. From students' reflections and papers, it is apparent that much of what they know about China is outdated or misguided by the media. It is important to keep in mind that dislike of the actions of a government should not be reflected on its people. As future teachers, not only can they increase their ICM and antiracist attitudes, but they can inform students and their families about it when discussions of anti-Chinese discrimination come up.

While most of our participants have shown progression toward becoming more interculturally mature, Camille did not. We believe we could have encouraged her to reflect and expand her worldview more deeply. In her journal entries and papers, it is evident that Camille did not have a framework beyond her own frame of reference to make sense of what she was seeing and experiencing. She seemed to fall in the category that Burford (2004) warned about with reinforcing stereotypes. The fact that Camille did not reference ethical frameworks certainly indicates that we, the instructors, need to put more emphasis on the frameworks and provide more scaffolding and practice in applying the frameworks. We will also need to establish a more direct connection to non-consequentialism and consequentialism. We can do this by being more specific in requiring students to respond directly to the frameworks in their observations and discussions and having individual discussions with students.

Another issue that seemed to not be present in Camille's responses was motivation. Mezirow (1997) underscored that people need to be motivated to change their thinking and outlines that "we have a strong tendency to reject ideas that fail to fit our preconceptions, labeling those ideas as unworthy of consideration—aberrations, nonsense, irrelevant, weird or mistaken" (p.

5). On further analysis of Camille's responses, there did not seem to be any motivation to expand her thinking. In fact, she seemed to thrive on being the expert on deaf education and emphasized the 'deficiencies' with it in China. Camille's worldview did not move beyond her own reality. In some ways, the visit to the School for the Deaf almost shut down Camille's ability to develop different frames of reference completely. She clearly took the view that the United States was vastly superior to China in terms of deaf education. While this might be the case, we could have pushed her further in understanding the context of the country. While special education is a relatively new movement in China, rather than seeing it merely as "behind" the United States, the more interesting question we should have asked was "Why is deaf education taught the way it is in China? What are the societal factors that have led to the way it is treated in China as compared to the U.S.?" In hindsight, we should have engaged students in a more formal discussion of special education using the various ethical frameworks. Perhaps that would have helped Camille understand the context more.

To become an antiracist and experience a paradigm shift in one's everyday life is not easy and typically does not happen overnight. A successful teacher education program needs to have antiracist and antibias education weaved throughout the entire program. Well-planned study abroad programs could be one approach, among many, to achieve this goal. We end our chapter with a powerful note from Sadie:

> The whole trip really reinforced the idea for me that love and hate only grow on what you feed them. We can choose to make remarks and judgments on a country which we've never been to and people we've never met based upon the information we gather from our point of view. This creates an enemy out of an idea and a fight out of a misunderstanding. On the other hand, we can choose to save these thoughts until we've talked to the people who live, thrive, grow, and continue to develop in this culture. This creates a friend out of a foreigner and cooperation of mutual understanding.

NOTE

1. It should be noted that Sadie's comments were made before there was any media attention on the Uighurs (also spelled Uyghurs) and "re-education" camps.

REFERENCES

Bennett, J. M., & Bennett, M. J. (2004). Developing intercultural sensitivity. In D. Landis, J. M. Bennett, & M. J. Bennett (Eds.), *The Handbook of intercultural training* (pp. 146–165). Sage Publications.

Blake-Campbell, B. (2014). More than just a sampling of study abroad: Transformative possibilities at best. *The Community College Enterprise, 20*, 60–71.

Brislin, R., & Kim, E. (2003). Cultural diversity in people's understanding and uses of time. *Applied Psychology, 52*(3), 363–382. http://doi.org/10.1111/1464-0597.00140

Burford, G. (2004). The nuts and bolts of site visits. *Religious Studies News: AAR Edition, 19*(4), v–xiv.

Clarke, I., Flaherty, T., Wright, N., & McMillen, R. (2009). Student intercultural proficiency from study abroad programs. *Journal of Marketing Education, 31*(2), 173–181. https://doi.org/10.1177/0273475309335583

Cushner, K., & Chang, S. (2015). Developing intercultural competence through overseas student teaching: Checking our assumptions. *Intercultural Education, 26*(3), 165–178. https://doi.org/10.1080/14675986.2015.1040326

DeLoach, S. B., Kurt, M. R., & Oliktsky, N. (2021). Duration matters: Separating the impact of depth and duration in study abroad programs. *Journal of Studies in International Education, 25*(1), 100–118. https://doi.org/10.1177/1028315319887389

Donnelly-Smith, L. (2009). Global learning through short-term study abroad. *Peer Review, 11*(4), 12–15.

Eichelberger, L. (2007). SARS and New York's Chinatown: The politics of risk and blame during an epidemic of fear. *Social Science & Medicine, 65*, 1284–1295.

Engle, L. (2013). The rewards of qualitative assessment appropriate to study abroad. *Frontiers: The Interdisciplinary Journal of Study Aboard, 22*, 111–126. https://doi.org/10.36366/frontiers.v22i1.321

Gaia, A. C. (2015). Short-term faculty-led study abroad programs enhance cultural exchange and self-awareness. *The International Education Journal: Comparative Perspectives, 14*(1), 21–31.

Gambino, G., & Hashim, S. M. (2016). In their own words: Assessing global citizenship in a short-term study-abroad program in Bangladesh. *Journal of Political Science Education, 12*(1), 15–29. https://doi.org/10.1080/15512169.2015.1063438

Gao, G., & Gudykunst, W. B. (1990). Uncertainty, anxiety, and adaptation. *International Journal of Intercultural Relations, 14*(3), 301–317.

Hill, J. (2005). Teaching for transformation: Insights from Fiji, India, South Africa, and Jamaica. *Teaching Theology & Religion, 8*(4), 218–231. http://doi.10.1111/j.1467-9647.2005.00248.x

Hoggan, C., & Cranton, P. (2015). Promoting transformative learning through reading. *Journal Of Transformative Education, 13*(1), 6–25. http://doi.10.1177/1541344614561864

Husu, J., Toom, A., & Patrikainen, S. (2008). Guided reflection as a means to demonstrate and develop student teachers' reflective competencies. *Reflective Practices, 9*(1), 37–51. https://doi.org/10.1080/14623940701816642

Hutchison, A., & Rea, T. (2011). Transformative learning and identity formation on the "smiling coast" of West Africa. *Teaching and Teacher Education, 27*(3), 552–559. http://doi.10.1016/j.tate.2010.10.009

Jeung, R., Horse, A. J. Y., & Cayanan, C. (2021). *Stop AAPI hate national report*. https://stopaapihate.org/wp-content/uploads/2021/05/Stop-AAPI-Hate-Report-National-210506.pdf

King, P. M., & Baxter Magolda, M. B. (2005). A developmental model of intercultural maturity. *Journal of College Student Development, 46*, 571–592. http://doi.10.1353/csd.2005.0060

Krieger, L. (1965). Kant and the crisis of natural law. *Journal of the History of Ideas 26*(2), 191–210. https://doi.org/10.2307/2708227

Ladson-Billings, G. (2014). Culturally relevant pedagogy 2.0: Aka. the remix. *Harvard Education Review, 84*(1), 74–84. https://doi.org/10.17763/haer.84.1.p2rj131485484751

Lee, G. B. (2017). Diseased and demented: The Irish, the Chinese, and racist representation. *Journal of Global Cultural Studies, 12*. https://doi.org/10.4000/transtexts.1011

Lee, S. J., Wong, N.-W. A., & Alvarez, A. N. (2009). The model minority and the perpetual foreigner: Stereotypes of Asian Americans. In N. Tewari & A. N. Alvarez (Eds.), *Asian American psychology: Current perspectives* (pp. 69–84). Routledge/Taylor & Francis Group.

Mezirow, J. (1997). Transformative learning: Theory to practice. *New Directions for Adult & Continuing Education, 1997*(74), 5–10.

Moseley, C., Reeder, S., & Armstrong, N. (2008). "I don't eat white": The transformational nature of student teaching abroad. *Curriculum & Teaching Dialogue, 10*(1/2), 55–71.

Paige, M., Fry, G., Stallman, E., Josić, J., & Jon, J. E. (2009). Study abroad for global engagement: The long-term impact of mobility experiences. *Intercultural Education, 20*(S1), S29–S44. https://doi.org/10.1080/14675980903370847

Perez, R. J., Shim, W., King, P. M., & Baxter Magolda, M. B. (2015). Refining King and Baxter Magolda's model of intercultural maturity. *Journal of College Student Development, 56*(8), 759–776. https://doi.org/10.1353/csd.2015.0085

Ritz, A. A. (2011). The educational value of short-term study abroad programs as course components. *Journal of Teaching in Travel & Tourism, 11*, 164–178. https://doi.org/10.1080/15313220.2010.525968

Sachau, D., Brasher, N., & Fee, S. (2009). Three models for short-term study abroad. *Journal of Management Education, 34*(5), 645–670. https://doi.org/10.1177/1052562909340880

Sandel, M. J. (2009). *Justice: What's the right thing to do?* Farrar, Straus and Giroux.

Shackleton, R. (1972). The greatest happiness of the greatest number: The history of Bentham's phrase. *Studies on Voltaire and the Eighteenth Century, 90*, 1461–1482.

Shiveley, J., & Misco, T. (2015). Long-term impacts of short-term study abroad: Teacher perceptions of preservice study abroad experiences. *The Interdisciplinary Journal of Study Abroad, 26*, 107–120. https://doi.org/10.36366/frontiers.v26i1.361

Sleeter, C., & Thao, Y. (2007). Guest editors' introduction: Diversifying the teaching force. *Teacher Education Quarterly, 34*(4), 3–8. https://doi:10.2307/23479107

Spencer, S. E., & Tuma, K. (Eds.). (2002). *The guide to successful short-term programs abroad*. NAFSA: Association of International Educators.

Stachowski, L. L. (2001). Enhancing international student teaching experiences. *Education, 112*(3), 347–351.

Terzuolo, E. R. (2018). Intercultural development in study abroad: Influence of student and program characteristics. *Intercultural Journal of Intercultural Relations, 65*, 86–95. https://doi.org/10.1016/j.ijintrel.2018.05.001

Vande Berg, M. (2014). Student learning abroad: Three stories we tell. *International Educator, 28*(1), 52–55.

Vatalaro, A., Szente, J., & Levin, J. (2015). Transformative learning of pre-service teachers during study abroad in Reggio Emilia, Italy: A case study. *Journal of the Scholarship of Teaching and Learning, 15*(2), 42–55.

Walters, C., Charles, J., & Bingham, S. (2017). Impact of short-term study abroad experiences on transformative learning: A comparison of programs at 6 weeks. *Journal of Transformative Education, 15*(2), 103–121. https://doi.org/10.1177%2F1541344616670034

Wen, J., Aston, J., Liu, X., & Ying, T. (2020). Effects of misleading media coverage on public health crisis: A case of the 2019 novel coronavirus outbreak in China. *Anatolia, 31*, 331–336. http://dx.doi.org/10.1080/ 13032917.2020.1730621

Wilson, A. H. (1982). Cross-cultural experiential learning for teachers. *Theory into Practice, 21*(3), 184–192.

Yin, R. K. (2018). *Case study research and applications: Design and methods* (6th ed.). Sage.

About the Editors

Gilda Martínez-Alba, Ed.D., is the assistant dean in the College of Education at Towson University, where she has worked for the past 15 years. Her research revolves around asset-based literacy instruction for multilingual learners integrating technology and social-emotional learning (SEL) as well as advocating for underrepresented students in the field of education. It is reflected in her publications, for example, *English U.S.A. Every Day*, which has sold over 6,000 copies around the world, and most recently *Social-Emotional Learning in the English Language Classroom*, which was just published through TESOL Press. She was the Provost Fellow for Diversity and Inclusion, where she created an online Diversity and Inclusion Tool Kit and an onboarding plan for faculty and staff. She cochaired the Latinx Faculty and Staff Association for eight years where she developed a platform for faculty to engage in research across colleges and gain mentors. She helped lead the Diversity Faculty Fellows Committee mentoring faculty in evolving inclusive syllabi. Furthermore, she was on a committee that developed the university's Diversity Strategic Plan and is now helping lead the College of Education to develop and implement their Diversity, Equity, and Inclusion plan. Last, at UMBC, she served on the Maryland Early Childhood Leadership Program Advisory Committee that helps develop and support a diversity of strong leaders equipped to lead innovation and change in systems, policies, and legislation for positive change.

Luis Javier Pentón Herrera, Ph.D., served as the 38th president of Maryland TESOL in 2018–2019. He currently serves as assistant professor at the University of Warsaw and as coordinator of the Graduate TESOL Certificate at the George Washington University. In addition, he serves as the Social Responsibility Interest Section Co-Chair (2021–2022) at TESOL

International Association. Dr. Pentón Herrera's current research projects include: exploring the language and literacy experiences of adolescent and adult Indigenous students from Latin America; exploring adolescent and adult students with limited or interrupted formal education (SLIFE); SEL, emotions, and well-being in language and literacy education; and autoethnography and storytelling. His latest books include *Critical storytelling: Multilingual immigrants in the United States* (with Ethan Tính Trinh; 2021), *Social-emotional learning in the English language classroom: Fostering growth, self-care, and independence* (with Gilda Martínez-Alba; 2021), *The Maryland TESOL handbook for educators of English learners* (with Drew Fagan and Sherry Lyons; 2021), and *English and students with limited or interrupted formal education: Global perspectives on teacher preparation and classroom practices* (2022). To learn more about Dr. Pentón Herrera, please visit his website https://luispenton.com/

Afra Ahmed Hersi, Ph.D., is the interim dean of the School of Education at Loyola University Maryland and professor in Literacy Teacher Education. Dr. Hersi has published research in the areas of immigration and education, literacy, language development for bilingual learners, culturally and linguistically responsive practice, and teacher education. Her focus is on academic opportunities for culturally and linguistically diverse students and research that expands the educational and life opportunities of marginalized children, their families, and communities. Her research has appeared in a number of journals, including *Teachers and Teaching, Educational Planning, Bilingual Research Journal, Career Development Quarterly,* and *Intercultural Education*. More recently, she served as coeditor of *PDS Partners: Bridging Research to Practice—Leveraging PDS Partnerships to Cultivate Equity in Education.*

About the Contributors

Zachary T. Barnes is an assistant professor of special education in the Teaching and Learning Department at Austin Peay State University in Clarksville, TN. He studies executive function, reading development, and reading disabilities.

Dr. Benita R. Brooks is the assistant dean of Diversity, Equity, and Inclusion and an associate professor of Literacy in the College of Education. She is the 2022 recipient of Sam Houston State University's David Payne Academic Community Engagement Award. In 2020, 66 teacher candidates completed a diversity certificate program that she created. In 2021, she collaborated with the College of Criminal Justice to create DEEDS: Diversity Education, Engagement, Development & Support, a campus-wide diversity certificate program. Her research interests involve education preparation programs preparing P-12 teacher candidates to implement culturally proficient and restorative practices in the classroom and community.

Jaime Coyne, Ph.D., is an associate professor of Teaching and Learning at Sam Houston State University. Her research interest has included preservice teaching preparation, self-efficacy, content-area literacy, and technology. She has received several awards including SHSU College of Education Faculty Excellence in Teaching Award, Active Learning Teaching Fellowship, and the Warren Faculty Holocaust Fellowship.

Danné E. Davis, Ph.D., is an associate professor at Montclair State University. Her scholarship centers on diversity and inclusion, the arts as pedagogy, and teacher education. These topics inform her numerous publications, presentations, and workshops. Dr. Davis's current research involves increasing elementary teacher candidates' awareness of and responsiveness to LGBTQ+ diversity. Using music and song to teach about the Black experience is another scholarly focus. Dr. Davis is the recipient of numerous awards and special recognitions.

Dr. Marisol Diaz uses critical race theory and a Marxist analysis of class to study correlations between socioeconomic class and academic achievement in elementary education, focusing on Hispanic/Chican@/Mexican populations. Her research areas include critical social justice issues in education, critical pedagogy, critical theory, and critical literacy. Dr. Diaz taught elementary school for seven years in the beautiful borderland of El Paso, Texas. In 2015, Dr. Diaz won the National Multicultural Educator award, an award that highlights educators that promote equity and multiculturalism in their classrooms. Dr. Diaz continues to work in her community, supporting teachers, parents, and students.

Nancy P. Gallavan, Ph.D., is professor emerita at University of Central Arkansas, per course instructor at Missouri State University, and instructional coach. Nancy's expertise includes teacher education, classroom assessments, cultural competence, online teaching and learning, and social studies education. Nancy has authored and/or edited 200+ peer-reviewed publications, including 20+ books. Active in ATE, Nancy is past president, distinguished member, distinguished mentor, and distinguished teacher educator. Nancy has received awards for teaching, scholarship, service, and diversity and inclusion from UCA, UCA College of Education, AERA, and Kappa Delta Pi as co-counselor and inaugural member of the KDP Eleanor Roosevelt Legacy Chapter.

Sumi Hagiwara, Ph.D., is acting associate dean for academic affairs and associate professor in the Department of Teaching and Learning in the College of Education and Human Services at Montclair State University. Her research includes computer science/STEM education, teacher preparation and parent engagement, and the role of culture and language in learning. Her work has been published in the *Journal of Research in Science Teaching*, *Cultural Studies of Science Education*, *International Journal of Science Education*, and *Education and Urban Society*.

Tori Hollas, Ph.D., is an associate professor in the School of Teaching and Learning at Sam Houston State University in Texas, where she teaches graduate courses. To date, Dr. Hollas's research has focused on novice teacher induction, preservice and inservice teacher preparation, and the evaluation of teacher candidates. Additional research has focused on the relationship between high-quality feedback and its link to student performance, value-added measures of teacher effectiveness, and the technical properties of several different gauges of teaching quality, including their ability to predict student outcomes.

Dr. Tonya D. Jeffery is an assistant professor of science education, social justice, and equity in the Department of Urban Education at the University of Houston-Downtown (UHD). She has served in various roles in public schools and higher education for 16 years. Dr. Jeffery's scholarship focuses on STEM teacher preparation, teaching science through the critical lens of social justice and equity, and culturally relevant pedagogy; as well as, an evolving focal point on social justice issues at the intersectionality of gender, race, and class, as it relates to women in academia. She also serves on ATE's diversity and equity committee.

Matthew Kruger-Ross, Ph.D., is an associate professor in the Department of Educational Leadership and Higher Education Administration. He teaches graduate courses on educational technology, curriculum, and research methodologies. Matthew's research interests include the philosophy of education and technology and its impact on educational practice, curriculum theory as it relates to teaching and being a teacher, and the intersection of philosophy of education and the hermeneutic phenomenology of Martin Heidegger.

Mae Lane, Ed.D., is an associate professor in the School of Teaching and Learning at Sam Houston State University in Texas, where she teaches undergraduate and graduate courses. Her research has focused on mentoring, preservice teachers, and content literacy.

Dr. Xiaoming Liu is an associate professor and Graduate Program director in the Department of Elementary Education at Towson University. Her research interests include literacy studies in international settings, reading processes of Chinese heritage language learners, children's literature, young children's biliteracy development, and diversity and equity in teacher education. Her work has been published as a number of book chapters and in various peer-reviewed journals. She is the state representative of the Field Council of the Literacy Research Association (LRA) (2017–2020). She also serves as co-chair of LRA's International Innovative Community Group (2009–2012) and is currently on the Steering Committee.

Dr. Ashley Lucas is an associate professor and Graduate Program director in the Department of Secondary and Middle School Education at Towson University. Her research interests focus on social studies, global education, and issues of social justice. She received her Ph.D. in Curriculum and Instruction from Indiana University Bloomington. In the past, she has served as the Program chair of the College and University Faculty Assembly (CUFA) and as chair of the International Assembly (IA).

Morna McDermott McNulty, Ph.D., is a professor in the College of Education at Towson University. Her teaching and research focus on the intersections among arts-based inquiry, social justice, and public education. She has worked in and with public schools for over 30 years. Her published books include *The Left-Handed Curriculum: Empowering Teachers through Creativity (2013)*, *The Activists Handbook for the Education Revolution* (2015), and *Blood's Will: Speculative Fiction, Identity, and Inquiry of Currere (2018)*. She has authored or co-authored over 30 peer-reviewed articles and 25 book chapters. She is also co-producer of the documentary *Voices of Baltimore: Life under Segregation* (2019).

Ramona T. Pittman, Ph.D., is an associate professor at Texas A&M University. She has seven years of PreK-12 teaching experience in Title 1 settings, and she has over 15 years of teacher preparation experience. She has served as a content advisor for literacy exams focused on initial teacher certification and has written literacy curriculum. Dr. Pittman understands that teachers must create and advocate for equitable learning experiences for all students. At her previous institution, she co-chaired the President's Commission on Equity. Dr. Pittman has published her research in numerous venues and has presented at several international, national, and regional conferences.

Laurie Rabinowitz is an assistant professor of Education Studies at Skidmore College. She holds an Ed.D. from Teachers College, Columbia University, an M.A. in Education Leadership from New York University and a M.S. in Special Education from Hunter College. Her research interests include teacher perspectives on inclusive practices, the representation of disability identity in children's literature, supporting teachers in developing critical literacy teaching practices and the cross-pollination of Universal Design for Learning and Culturally Sustaining Pedagogy.

Laura Renzi, Ph.D., is a professor of English Education in the Department of Secondary Education at WCUPA where she is also the Department chair. Her doctoral research looked at teacher education and teachers' beliefs, with specific attention paid to how teachers come to an understanding of what teaching English Language Arts is and how preservice teachers want to present themselves as a teacher in the classroom. Laura works to push the preservice teachers to disrupt texts and/or challenge the traditional white canonical literature that continues to dominate the secondary English classroom.

Dr. Sarah M. Straub is an associate professor and antibias, antiracist educator in progress. While teaching K-12 in southwest Houston, she earned her doctoral degree from the University of Houston in curriculum and instruction with a focus on social justice education. Straub is an award-winning educator who is most proud of her student-driven publications. She values critical pedagogy and social justice education, which is embedded throughout her courses and in her activism with student groups like the Bilingual Education Student Organization. Additionally, Straub serves on the board for the Texas chapter of the National Association for Multicultural Education.

Amy Tondreau is an assistant professor of Elementary Literacy at the University of Maryland, Baltimore County. She holds an Ed.D. in Curriculum & Teaching from Teachers College, Columbia University. She previously worked as a staff developer and writer for the Teachers College Reading and Writing Project, co-director of the Summer Literacy Clinic at Rhode Island College, and an elementary classroom teacher. Her research focuses on teachers' and students' literacy identities, critical literacy in children's literature and writing pedagogy, professional learning communities, and the cross-pollination of Universal Design for Learning and Culturally Sustaining Pedagogy in literacy teaching and learning.

Dr. Brian Uriegas is an assistant professor in the Department of Human Services and Educational Leadership at Stephen F. Austin State University where he teaches in their M.Ed. and Ed.D. programs. Prior to his arrival at SFA, Dr. Uriegas spent 17 years as a teacher, coach, and principal in Texas public schools. Dr. Uriegas holds a doctorate in Educational Leadership from Texas A&M University-Kingsville. Brian's research interests are centered on rural education with a focus on postsecondary readiness, students of poverty, career and technical education, diversity, equity, and inclusion, school leadership and advancement for Latinx students and faculty in higher education.